Praise for *Fly Over D[*

MW00478690

"I very much enjoyed reading your book about flying all over Down Under. You have a very lively style that makes people, situations, and even landscapes come alive."

—Walter Hoebling, published poet,
Professor, University of Graz, Austria

"Michelee Cabot's *Fly Over Down Under*, describing how she and husband Hal circumnavigated the entire continent of Australia, hit the interest jackpot. Michelee is a gifted writer. I vicariously enjoyed her adventure Down Under. I learned a great deal about people, places, history, all the basic ingredients that comprise a typical travel book. What sets this one apart is a spritely sense of humor, her profound passion, and her knowledge about airplane piloting, a world I never experienced."

—Earle Winderman, PhD,
Retired Vice President Lincoln University,
BA Comparative Literature

"*Fly Over Down Under* is a truly modern-day adventure that most of us will never experience. Michelee Cabot tells the tale of their trip with a great sense of humor, an astounding vocabulary, and with a wonderful study of the history of each aspect of their air-minded route. Very enjoyable and enlightening."

—Willis Allen,
President Allen Airways Flying Museum
and Crystal Pier Hotel and Cottages, Inc.

"As one who has always wanted to see all of the various, and dramatically different, areas of Australia for many years, I was able to take such a trip while reading Michelee's *Fly Over Down Under*. Plus in later years, after becoming a pilot, it made the book even more interesting due to just enough of the pilot's jargon and experiences while on this 'flying trip' to make the reading experience twice as delightful. Never did the 'read' lag due to a good dose of humor mixed with an ever-changing view of Australia."

—Jim Swickard,
Owner of the Hacienda de los Santos
in Álamos, a five-star boutique hotel

FLY
OVER
DOWN
UNDER

Australian Adventures by
Single-Engine Airplane

Michelee Morgan Cabot

Cover photo: The Twelve Apostles is a famous Australian coastal landmark at the eastern end of the Great Australian Bight.

Back cover author photo by Juan Pablo Garza Mouriño.

Fly Over Down Under: Australian Adventures by Single-Engine Airplane

Published by Wheatmark®
1760 East River Road, Suite 145
Tucson, Arizona 85718 USA
www.wheatmark.com

ISBN: 978-1-62787-301-7 (color paperback)
ISBN: 978-1-62787-337-6 (color hardcover)
ISBN: 978-1-62787-271-3 (black and white paperback)
ISBN: 978-1-62787-272-0 (ebook)
LCCN: 2015936742

rev201501

Hey! Vera! come fly with me ☺ ∑ Warmst, Michelle July 2018

For Hal—my editor, best friend, and lifetime copilot.
For my fellow pilot Ninety-Nines and my amazing Aero Club of
New England, first aero club of the western hemisphere.
For our tried and true Aussie leader.
For our dear fellow adventurers.
And for our very wonderful children—
may you find your own kind of flying.

Contents

FOREWORD

by Bill Cox

As one who was fortunate enough to make twenty-two aircraft delivery flights from the US to Australia back in the '90s and early 2000s, I often wished there were some kind of guidebook for the sites I overflew at 140 to 220 knots. There probably was, but I never found it in my fifteen years of travel to every major city in the land Down Under (do Australians call the rest of the world Up Over?), delivering everything from Twin Commanders, Skymasters, and Cessna 414s to Mooneys, Saratoga HPs, and Bonanzas.

I would have enjoyed a book that helped impart the sense of the country and points of interest rather than a simple been there/done that account of places and things.

Now there is exactly that.

Michelee Cabot's new nonfiction work, *Fly Over Down Under*, is a fun read about a caravan of Skyhawks and Cherokees that toured Australia in 1997 and visited many of the places I overflew so casually a few years ago, too busy trying to make money to really enjoy what I was seeing.

Michelee is perhaps especially qualified to write a guide-book such as this. In fairness, this isn't a guidebook, though it does detail the many stops and adventures Michelee and Hal Cabot had on their five-thousand-nautical-mile air trek around a country roughly the size of the United States with a population around the size of New York City's.

Michelee grew up an Air Force brat, living all over the world—Philippines, Japan, Europe, and numerous US bases. It was perhaps only natural that she would someday embrace aviation and fall in love with the sky.

Michelee writes with a breezy, casual style that encourages you to read the next chapter and the one after that, thirty in all, with engaging descriptions of the people and places that give Australia a certain mystical sense of adventure.

In the interest of full disclosure, I should admit that I've been friends with Michelee and Hal Cabot for over twenty years. Through most of that time, they lived in Massachusetts; I used to stop through on my way across the Atlantic to Europe, the Middle East, and Africa. They're both pilots and they're avid Cessna fans, having owned everything from a Skylane and a Turbo Centurion to their current Pressurized Centurion. Had they asked, I probably would have ferried their Cessna P210 seven thousand miles to Oz if they'd let me use it for a few weeks.

The Cabots have flown all over the world by airline. Their air caravan was their chance to see that remarkable country so far south and so much like the US, yet so different.

As Michelee wrote at the end of *Fly Over Down Under*, "I imagine it was inevitable. One day, years after learning to fly, off I went to ramble the world, bit by bit. And I wanted to share some of it with you, tell you how it was.

"Especially flying in Australia."

Senior editor of Plane & Pilot *magazine, Bill Cox began writing about airplanes in 1971. Since then, he's written some 2,200 articles. Bill began delivering aircraft internationally in 1978 and has made 211 trips to destinations in Europe, Africa, Australia, Asia, and the Middle East. He currently holds commercial, multi-engine, instrument, seaplane, glider, and helicopter ratings and has accumulated some 15,000 flying hours. He also holds twenty-seven FAI, world, and city-to-city speed records.*

PULLING IT TOGETHER

As I drew together threads of our Australian flying adventure—out of my head, notes, and aircraft log—some visions were more vivid: low flights over long stretches of beaches, slow circles over Ayers Rock—impressive, strong memories, some to be recounted at another time. But as I began the reweaving, it all flew up into full-color action—an exercise of fun flashbacks. Not all moments were grand and explosive, but each had some extraordinary quality that fixed itself forever in our minds' eyes. Never was it humdrum, not even the odd preflight and climbout, but the truly astonishing is what transformed Australia into, for us, a mystical Oz. It was exhilarating; it was eye-opening. It was a whipperoo of an adventure, our flying down under.

FLY
OVER
DOWN
UNDER

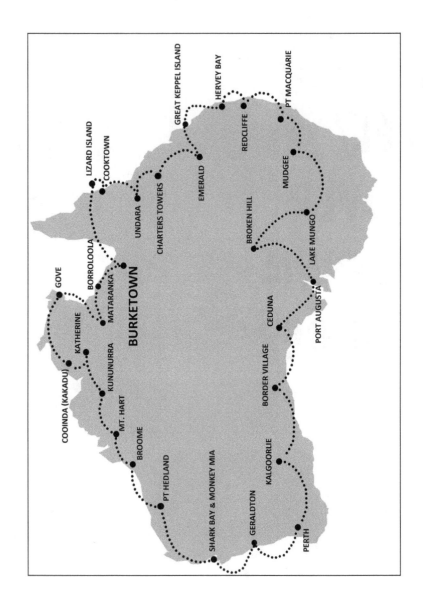

Trip route

1 DOWN UNDER

VIEWED FROM OUTER SPACE, we see Australia alone and apart on our planet, serenely placed on the vast sweep of the Pacific Ocean. Edged here and there with hopeful green, a huge span of scorched reddish earth dominates its wide expanse, a continent that lies mostly bare under fair skies. We are sometimes alerted to a great swirl of storms during its rainy season, and during dry months we watch impressive smoke banners stream out on shifting world air masses—telltale signs of agricultural burn-off or perhaps a great disaster. Our interest is passing. We tend not to notice or care much. It's way out of our way on our globe, disconnected from the rest of us among the seven seas.

Peering closely, we observe that its pale geology is thinly ringed by intense blues—the demarcation of surrounding oceans. At night, faintly indicating its place on the earth, a sketchy thread of lights outlines the continent, and along it the rare cluster of shining cities. There is the intriguing small glimmer of Alice Springs in the middle, but then the view scans way across the unrelieved blackness to the southwest coast. There, Perth seems a small superimposed distant galaxy, as does far-off Sydney to the southeast coast—and the few other coastal metropolises. In between, from fifty miles inland, there's nothing but the vaguest black. Blackness sometimes dusted with silver from the ambient light of the universe or from time to time brilliant blotches of outback wildfires. No techno-civilization—seemingly no civilization at all. (Except Alice.) Few but the indigenous Aborigines live out there, and they don't use much electricity.

When Robert O'Hara Burke and William John Wills assembled camels and heavy wagons on the south coast of Australia in 1860, setting out northward cross-lots to explore the uncharted interior—to Europeans a huge *terra incognita*—their goal was to reach the Gulf of Carpentaria. Some did make it, but in brutal hardships along the way they lost several luckless members of the team. Problems were unimagined and immense. Between dreadful rains, subsequent mud, starvation, and scorching heat, it was a doomed enterprise.

They had set out in two groups. Naively saying at start-up something like the equivalent of "meet you at the corner on the fifteenth," they headed out earnestly and enthusiastically—only to find themselves wrestling futilely against nature, often making only small, wretched advances. They never dreamed that inland there would be no handy navigable rivers. Huge boggy swamps oozed up to slog about in, and sometimes even float a boat in—but rivers? Not a one. Why, naturally there would be at least *one*, coursing down the middle—after all there were rivers emptying out to sea from the coasts. But no—no Mississippi here, no Rhine, no

Nile, no Amazon. Sadly, in the whole of their trek the only semblance of a waterway they would find would be the odd billabong—the visible manifestation of the braided river, a lanyard-like rope of erosion carved across the landscape. Most of the year billabongs, or ponds, are inaccessible and useless underground rivers where fluids seep hidden and unavailable. Often these billabongs emerge only during the "Wet" (rainy) season, tantalizing the thirsty Euro-immigrant. Still today they can madden desert-parched wayfarers. Most of that water is foul. And so the hapless explorers struggled and staggered, some to their deaths—Burke and Wills tragically missing their star-crossed rendezvous by a pitiful couple of hours, a place marked today by a tree and a sun-bleached sign. That's what happens when you have no maps. They should have checked with the Aborigines.

You see, Australian Aborigines have no maps. With no written language, they are said to use "songlines" to unerringly navigate their land, a memorized process of singing their tribes' boundaries to the next fellow up the line, matching up the edges of the territories. Quite a feat of intellect, when you think of it. They're said to use this method when they go "walkabout," which happens whenever the urge hits. Aborigines are infamous for being suddenly overcome by nomadic psychic promptings. Their heads seem to be programmed on a different plane. One day they simply get up without a word and leave jobsites or villages for whatever place and time is mandated by that inner voice. When it's over, they just show up one day, reappearing from wherever they were called to. Certainly days, could be weeks, often for months. Even years. Intriguing.

And annoying.

HOW WE GOT THERE

That inner voice. For some, it's wanderlust—a pull to the unfamiliar, to see around the curve in the road. Or the curve of the earth. For us it was a magazine page turned to an intriguing ad, and our own voice whispered seductively, "Aha . . . What's this?" It said, "Air Touring, Flying Down Under . . ."

Part of the allure of flying small airplanes is that you do indeed become one in heart with the bird. Wild vistas open up to you: wave-tossed seas, towering mountains, sun-topped clouded skies. Federal aviation regulations require that a constant awareness be kept on the world outside the cockpit—visual flight rules. No gluing your eyes to the panel's artificial horizon—no peering constantly at the turn indicator in front of you. Look *outside* to note a turning, banking aircraft. Skills must be acquired to incorporate an instrument scan along with your scenic touring, but this comes easily with the required hours of training and practice. It's not so hard. In no time you can become the blood-rushing union of "me, plane, sky."

But only if it's there, sleeping in your blood, waiting to be awakened. Try it. You'll find out quickly if it is.

And if it is, such sweet adventures can come. It can take you over.

When I think back on my early flying years, the remembrances of the predawn flights all alone from our little local airport are maybe my fondest. Mysterious nighttime, when ghosts swirl in graveyards and lights wink slowly on passing airliners high aloft.

The hours when highwaymen once caused laws against being abroad in the night, when curfews were applied for the protection of the innocent. Curfew, couvre-feu, or get thee inside, bolt the door, and shutter the windows. I would arise urgently and quietly in the dark, pulling on clothes, murmuring to my slumbering mate that I would be back soon. A peek into the kids' rooms to sense that all was well, and then I would rev up the VW and putter down the lonesome road for a couple of miles to where the plane was tied down. Fanning a flashlight preflight inspection over my bird's surfaces I checked the oil . . . Yes, all was as I had left it. An airfield at night . . . There's an exhilarating strangeness to be the only one there, alone in the absolute stillness, parked aircraft lined up waiting in their tie-downs. Always unnerving, the purring airport cat, Downwind, would suddenly glide out of the inky shadows like a wraith, padding silently, winding itself around my ankles as I moved around checking the tail, nose, and ailerons. Food? It suggested. Not me, little buddy.

Dawn would be a faint hint by the time I rolled for takeoff, not full and rosy until after diner coffee and a muffin at the next airport over. I would click the mic to turn on the runway lights, push the throttle forward, and climb out over the hidden landscape. An easterly heading would take me to the next airfield—a lightening sky revealing the runway. I would land and taxi up to the diner's back door. "How ya doin'?" greetings came from early workers inside . . . Winging back to home base and then driving back home, I grinned. Commuters had started filling up the roadway. But I had had my flight fix and was ready to rattle the pans—fry up the family bacon, scramble the eggs, and butter up the toast. What a great start to a super day.

"Everything go okay?" queried my sleepy-eyed husband with a hug. The boys were not interested.

So then. Hmm. An Australian aviation outfit offered to guide a convoy of pilots in rental airplanes, a sightseeing sortie (we dubbed it our "flyabout"). This gaggle of small planes would fly to faraway places: Perth of the first space-orbiting contact; Uluru of the ancient mystic mountain; Alice Springs; Kakadu; Captain Cook's Cooktown; the Great Barrier Reef.

So as the Aborigine is driven to get up and go "walk-about," Australia urged us too, to roam. Oh, we were hooked.

Seriously hooked—so much so that we formed a flying party three times around Australia—and still it beckons. This is mostly about the big trip, the monthlong circum-navigator. Two years before, our initial tour of two weeks had taken us from Sydney to points north and west. This had agreeably lifted the veil of mystery from Alice Springs and Uluru's Ayers Rock and had clarified the intriguing notion of the outback. This time, it would be the second in our trio of adventures.

2 And We Are There

Qantas Airways, an acronym for Queensland and Northern Territory Aerial Services, lifted us up and over the huge global distances to our adventure. An eighteen-hour flight—and there it appeared, the promising shape of Australia. Suddenly we were there.

Undeniably, there are delightful revelations at road level. So before hooking up with our flying troop, we stepped out in faith, rented a car, and started adventuring—timidly exiting from a downtown car rental garage into traffic, into what was for us the frightening wrong side of the road. Thus we forged our path from Sydney to Brisbane. It was on-the-job learning—ah, those adrenaline rushes while scuffing curbs, thwacking side mirrors . . . squeaks of panic while frantically unraveling strange road signs.

In a bit, we got it.

Motoring to Brisbane via the scenic inland route, we passed through pungent thick silvery-green eucalyptus forests (there are some five hundred species of this koala food) and lovely, wonderfully foreign landscapes. The byways of Australia's own hilly area, known funnily enough as "New England," wound through picturesque townships and tidy gardens lush with pleasingly exotic blossoms. We marveled that the only flowers we recognized were a rose and a petunia. Later we would discover the peculiar kangaroo paw blossom.

In a cozy café, we warily braved Aussie Vegemite. "Oh, do have some ma'am, you'll like it! It's a basic favorite here," coerced our waiter. *Not.* It was nasty stuff, obviously an acquired taste. Sort of an untoothsome spreadable bouillon. He grinned slyly, knowing full well the Yankee palate was untrained.

Then we learned about "bowsers." At a gas station leaned a big, hand-lettered sign stating, "Tell bowser NO at the counter." Okay, the dog was a pest where you pay, and if you buy a snack don't share it with him. Right? Well, actually no. The "bowser" is a gas pump, and NO meant "number." The pump number. No dog.

Candy-pink-and-gray parrots (galahs) grouped themselves in yattering lines on telephone wires like fluorescing pigeons—only there are no pigeons. No sparrows either. Instead, tiny green parakeets blew in flocks across the roads, the ill-fated pasting themselves to the radiator grille like sad, tattered butterflies. Magpies warbled liquid songs on the verges, instead of the raucous hopping crow.

We had surely slipped into a parallel world.

Brisbane—handsome, cosmopolitan, lively, and picturesque. And close to our tour-departure airport. Ferryboats crisscrossed the large harbor like buses; a Sunday farmers' market on a downtown quay bustled with food and art; a zoo offered a pleasing collection of birds, kangaroos, koalas, and fruit bats; the university put on excellent professional performances at a black-box theater—all reflections of the Australian warmth and spirit.

Brisbane, city on a sparkling harbor

Our tour had arranged a river-view city motel for us—a simple but charming accommodation. For creature comforts, Australians had it all over us Yanks. For example, at motels sans restaurants, we were not forgotten. They would *never* let us start our day without food. A cereal "brekkie" appeared through a discreet sliding window onto a handy inside shelf at the appointed hour. Through our drowsy wits we heard a little rasping sound and a tentative thunk, and in came our breakfast, a new spin on room service. And they had delicious ground "plunger coffee" in the rooms. At least they used to. I fear the crawling creep of American mediocrity may have made its way, and the aromatic brew of coffee *a la cafetière* may have morphed into dreary packets of instant caffeine kick-starts.

On our first flyabout two years earlier, we experienced a dreamlike dawn ballooning over the city. Steve Griffin, Australian Montgolfier Award winner for his 1994 trans-Australia accomplishment (the French Montgolfier brothers had been the first to hot air balloon) took us aloft—packing us into a wicker ballooning basket that arose from a dim predawn hospital yard (possibly a kick for patients to peer at) ending up miles away in a pasture of curious horses. As we began our drifting across the city, the sun artfully modeled the architecture of McMansions, "starter castles"—the economy was as rosy as the landscape. In the distance we spotted another balloon arising for the dawn look-see, suspended and drifting above the slowly awakening city, silence disturbed only by the occasional whooshing burst of gas flaming upward into the balloon, heating air to keep us aloft. Steve spotted a good countryside field, and down we slowly sank, touching earth like a thistle. Immediately, curious horses gathered around, and a magpie alit on our basket—warbling out a melodic greeting. Someone's pet? A captivating moment—but the pasture was so full of horse apples the chase car had to whisk us away from the champagne breakfast "en plein aire" to champagne flutes at a restaurant.

REDCLIFFE ARRIVAL

Having braved the highways calamity-free, we excitedly pulled into our tour's aerodrome. The group was gathering.

Leader Nick Sharpe—guide, pilot, certified mechanic, and owner of our little fleet of airplanes—greeted us warmly. Among our fellow travelers there were a couple of repeat pilots to hail—a lot of happy back thumping and hugging. Then we quickly fell in for sandwiches and the flight briefing. Eager to roll, we gathered charts and spread them out to study. Most importantly, we were each issued a GPS with every destination already entered. To save many hours of time, the journey's legs (point-to-point flights are called legs) had been drawn out for us, and to save the bulk of excess paper and unneeded information, those route legs were drawn on charts cut to show just the tour route.

We'd be covering thousands of miles, visiting special areas hardly seen by ground travelers—many places only seen by air—plus the usual tourist sights. It would be a full trip, and, we hoped, a rolling party. And so it was.

Mostly.

3 THE FIRST LEG

DESTINATION, HERVEY BAY

Having wrapped up insurance requirements—three successful takeoffs and landings to prove we probably wouldn't kill ourselves and sincerely embarrass Nick—we scrambled down out of the hangar ready room, checked over our single-engine aircraft, fired up, and taxied for takeoff. Nonchalant herons and blasé spoonbills languidly fed in little billabongs alongside the seaside runway, hardly moving as our engines roared past.

As we lined up for departure, Reggie, one of our jolly Aussies, boomed out over his radio, "All stations Redcliffe—*Here we go, here we go, here we go!*" gleefully breaking the tension. That's an Australian football rooting cheer—which became our theme cry. (Now, I need to tell you that in Australia you do *not* "root" for your team—you "barrack." To them, "root" means "*rut.*" So a girl does not "root" for her team—at least not usually. Or if so, she keeps it to herself.)

Oh, the elation of a new overview, a deliciously strange

new landscape, as we soared up to the sight of off-main-land islands and multihued blue waters. Now a little test—finding the checkpoints off to the left as we made our way up the coast. It was nice to have a radio frequency to consult our fellow pilots, especially since air traffic controllers spoke "Strine" or "Strahlian," tongue-in-cheek abbreviations for Australian, so unfamiliar to our Yankee ears.

The plan was to head north up the shoreline for an hour or so and then land at tourist mecca Hervey Bay for two nights. We were to join a whale watching boat tour at Platypus Bay to see breeding pods of globe-circling giant humpback whales. Here was shelter near this faraway landmass.

The area was utterly beautiful, tropical, and remote. But by virtue of its proximity to Brisbane, Hervey Bay's splendid beaches and migrating whale pods had become quite a draw, a resort destination with its own civilized settlement. Of course an attraction for world travelers required support networks; there were paved streets, strip malls, gas stations, and restaurants. Disappointingly just like home. What had I expected? "Roos" hopping down Main Street, boxing each other?

THE HUMPBACK WHALE

These agile, majestic creatures, often heavily barnacled and impressively scarred (anything that big has to scrape against things), have made Hervey Bay a regular stop on their annual migration to Antarctica after giving birth in the warm waters of North Queensland. It was astonishing how mothers and calves were comfortable with boats of gawkers—rolling, spouting, and breeching exuberantly, seemingly as charmed with us as we were with them. We snapped our fill of whale pictures along with touring Australians, some rowdy backpacking Japanese, and reticent Germans and Danes. We wondered what the parents of these Japanese kids were going to think when they saw their scions with us grinning Yanks, arms flung around each other, giggling.

I think they were pie-eyed. They did reek. It then became skewed. Over the intercom the captain announced, "Princess Diana has been killed in a car crash in Paris." Yes, our flyabout was that year . . . What a sudden ugly snapback to the world left behind. The moment was so shocking, so incongruous, so totally out of kilter, that we soon simply moved on beyond it and back into our adventure. But we will always remember where we were.

Mult-Hull to our portside

THE ENSEMBLE

Our group added eight to the international mix aboard the boat. There we were: Hal and me; the leader, Nick; two Danes; our two Aussies; and then Jerry, another Yank.

My husband, Hal, and I played alternating pilot and copilot roles, by leg. Since he took up flying, it had been our modus operandi—not that we weren't prone to backseating each other, but not to the point of blows. We were pleased with each other's accomplishments.

And then our two Danish pilots, Willem and his wife, Maartja, who had already done a flyabout the year before. He was an older settled sort, a heavy thick bulk of muscles with bulging calves—a barrel-torsoed pallid man, pale eyed with pinky pale skin. A double-wide, bald fireplug. She was younger—petite, lithe, and prettily auburn haired. Both were pilots, he instrument rated, she just licensed, and seemed very nice.

Sydney native Reggie was a short, fortyish, dark-haired, soft-bellied international banker, an accomplished tippler of postflight beers. His capacity for mirth and alcohol was extraordinary—it's said to be an Australian birthright. Maybe so . . . Our flights were generally one three-hour leg per day, before the rising heat thermals bumped us out of the sky. So upon reaching the day's destination, he would down a few and then do a marathon prowl just "to see what was out there." He also sucked red lollipops along the airways. When we landed he would merrily stick out a reddened tongue saying, "Look! My low bee-ah presh-ah warning light is annunciating!" And off we would dash to find a pub. Our ringleader. (When I muttered how hard it would be to keep up with his elbow bending, he became serious and said, "Ah dahlin', don't even try. That would be bad . . . I've been training for yee-ahs!") He was warm and friendly with expressive dark eyes and smile lines tracing years of mirth. An ace of a guy, crackling with good humor and intelligence, he entertained us with lurid tales of New Guinea where he had banking business, decrying the still-existent cannibals in their hinterlands. "You don't want to go to New Guinea," he pronounced. He was the type to grab adventure—one of which had been to challenge winds and weather to fly solo to Tasmania over pitching seas in howling winds. Not unusual conditions for that passage. Thinking about it made my palms sweat—with envy.

His mate Brad, a nonpilot landscaper (Australian men's pals are "mates") was equally good-humored. He was our company's stand-up comedian, blond and lanky, full of jokes and tales of mischief pulled on his mates, and near-legendary stories of some physician friends' escapades. He gave life to the "wobblehead" Indian doctor Panji-Panji, whose patients "would not rissen." He narrowed his blue eyes to slits, showing only black pupils, and spun tales of his Chinese business counterpart till we collapsed with mirth. Those two jump-started the mornings with TV cartoons "to start the day right." The quiet Danes were not used to all this, but were pleasant natured and spoke fluent English. They surely would adjust.

Now let me say a word about Jerry. Jerry was *sui generis.* An American megacorporation's computer tech, he was the archetypical IT expert with a streak of heavy introversion. No eye contact. He had "taciturn" down pat but seemed eager to fly and get with the game. He was superficially pleasant enough. But once en route, his reticence made us nervous. My imagination ran irrationally amok. Would he garrote someone in the night? I'm not sure of his upbring-ing, but he was stingy as hell with his travel cookies. We each had a little cockpit stash of nibbles for peckish moments. He never shared his, but he sure expected some of ours. And a small thing—it became irritating how at dinnertime he would announce that he "had to save room for dessert." Like, so what? We found ourselves bending over backward to be nice, hoping it would be catching. Just in case.

Back to the Danes. Confession: I was jumpy about Maartje. She was far too big eyed and focused on my tall good-looking husband. (He is actually quite yummy.) When we shook hands at our first get-to-know-ya drinks time, her fingers were telltale with a sexy skin softener, an attractiveness enhancer. Oh boy. Maybe she was tired of her old fireplug. Suddenly I wasn't looking forward so much to our group dynamics.

A cheery, "Night-night, see you early!" and we found our way to bed. The occasional peep and rustle from stirring critters called me into the lush tropical darkness, following half-lit walks along the inn's canal. Those curious sounds, and oh heck, a disturbing nidginess about the Danish siren. I talked some sense into myself, quietly returned to bed beside my mate ("Hmmpff, glad you're back"), and slept well.

Things change.

4 THE GREAT KEPPEL INCIDENT

WITH SUNRISE, WE EAGERLY hustled out of bed for the next leg. But uh-oh. Low fog was reported at our next stopover, the Whitsundays' Brampton Island resort. So then, a change of plans? We are VFR, a visual flight rules group. "Ah, no dramas. It'll be all right, we'll head instead to Great Keppel Island!" said Nick reassuringly. "It's sunny there . . . I'll arrange it."

"Oh, no," murmured Willem, anxiety bunching his wide pink forehead. His pale eyes squinched tightly. He had been there just the year before, and the approach had quite shaken him. "Ah, no worries," Nick scoffed airily. "The runway has fine new bitumen and it's nice and long. A great place—you'll be fine, you'll love it." He was the Man, the trustworthy head of it all. So we fired up our engines and started the short hop up the line and over the water, just off Rockhampton, Hal and I trailing last for takeoff.

It was an easy, smooth, pretty flight, the uplifting kind that reaffirms your decision to learn how to do this thing.

Out of breathtaking bright aqua waters, the hilly island arose in front of us. And sure enough, around the hill and into the clear came the airstrip, nestled between two ridges. With Hal at the yoke, we overflew Great Keppel to check the runway. It was indeed nice and long, black and wide, freshly marked. We observed a plane parked beside the strip near the rollout end, facing into the hill. Okay then, that's where we tie down.

The UNICOM came alive with "Sierra Charlie Uniform" (that's us), "the last three hundred feet of runway is closed." We acknowledged with a "roger," figuring that area was guarded for Ansett Australia's commuter movements. Great Keppel was a popular resort. What else?

We flew the downwind snug to the outside of the hill, losing sight of the runway momentarily, but we surely knew where it was. Right enough, it popped back into view as we continued the downwind, in plenty of time for a comfortable turn to final approach. An inside track alongside the runway to keep it always within sight would also have been possible, but that would have made a mighty tight U-turn to land—not our preference. Pulses racing, we turned base out over the water. Final approach was fairly long; we wanted plenty of room to comfortably line up for the touchdown zone, our modus operandi at new airfields. Because of the announced advisory, we needed to land close to the numbers. We adjusted power coming in over the resort's harbor beach (winds quite calm—"three knots gusting to five," drily announced Nick on his handheld radio). Hal put her down gently, making sure to be short of the announced no-ops area. Nicely done. And there was the very resort itself, off to the side.

We were directed to parking at a wind sock marked by

giant parking cones, big fat things I think peculiar to Australia. The group was already there and turned hollow eyes to us. There was a lot of shifting from foot to foot. Guess what—of course there was no parking up there alongside the runway. That was the Danes' plane—but not exactly *parked.*

What had happened is that Willem had blown the landing horribly, seriously pranging their Cessna, careening off the runway most ungracefully, to understate it. A horrible thing.

According to Brad, the Dane was indeed skittish about landing at Keppel. He totally clutched. In his trembling fear he made a weaving, bobbling, out-of-control approach (Maartje must have been scared witless)—yawing, billowing, sinking sideways and forward, finally whacking that fresh blacktop a few times as he bounced and zigzagged madly up the strip striking the ground *sideways*—curled the prop two ways—a catastrophic engine stop with impressive gashes in the pavement.

He ripped off the nose gear, bent up the two main gear, beat up the wingtips, and let's see . . . what else. Oh yes—*bent down the front seat tracks*—not easy to do. Only a rivet or two remained uncompromised.

The magic carpet had rolled itself up. But they themselves, thank God, were unhurt. And amazingly, no fire.

There's a pithy saying in flying, "Any landing you can walk away from is a good landing. And any landing where you can use the airplane again afterward is a great landing." Well, they walked away—but left an unusable craft in their wake.

In spite of the Incident, or rather because of it, the rest of us threw ourselves into a rollicking golf game on the resort's rudimentary seven-hole course overhung by lush trees—significantly without the Danes and without leader Nick. Colorful birds flickered about—warbling currawongs, screeching lorikeets, magpies ringing out advisories like carillons, little honey-suckers, and big-headed kookaburras. One of the kookaburras dove at Hal's head, the aggressive cheeky thing "laughing" as he buzzed him. (Note: bird color and decibel levels are significantly greater in Australia than back home.) We were able to put the Incident to the backs of our minds for a pleasant hour or two.

On the way to some soothing elbow bending, we passed Maartje and Willem sitting out on their room's little terrace. I was glad to see with my own eyes that they were unhurt. Rattled, demoralized, and certainly depressed, but unhurt. I declared my relief to them with an invitation to join us at the bar, but, unsurprisingly, they did not wish to. Though wildly curious to know what had happened, I think none of us wanted to have to commiserate. Of course if conditions had been adverse, it would have been different. At our nineteenth hole, we spoiled a XXXX beer or two (known as 4X). Reggie chortled, "Queenslanders? They

drink XXXX because they can't spell b-e-e-r." A regional joke.

So aside from *that*, the resort was perfect—a place of gracefully curved and flowered walkways and terraces, romantically shaded by towering tropical trees growing to the edges of soft crescent beaches. There were very few people at

Kookaburra

the resort, making for a pleasantly exclusive and quiet retreat.

But surely not dull. Some Euro-chic strolled by, swinging bosom-free, topless. "Gloriously built," our guys commented—her naked breasts adding a surreal touch to a day already out of whack. Show-off.

Segue to dinner. We sat down to palate-engaging *haute cuisine*, but no happy patter. Nick sat mute, stunned and numbed by this maintenance disaster. (A year later, however, by some profound legerdemain, the aircraft was completely mended and airborne again.) The Danes sat stiffly silent, mortified. The rest of us munched along, skillfully pretending nothing was amiss. (On the way into the dining room Brad had leaned toward us and murmured *sotto voce*, with dry humor, "Remember . . . Do *not* mention the War!")

Predawn the next day, the Danes crept out before we could see them again—to tour Australia by car. (I wasn't sorry.) They had promised Nick they would see him at the end of the four weeks to make good on their damages. Good thing, for wouldn't you know—our leader was *self*-insured. *Not* carrying hull insurance—hard to get and virtually unaffordable down under. (We heard later they had paid up as promised.)

So much for those first-day required "circuits and bumps."

So there we were, up early for a head start to Undara, home of the lava tubes, wondering what on earth could happen next. What a beginning . . .

The convoy had shrunk. We were now three aircraft, six people.

5 To Undara

EN ROUTE, A TOP-OFF

What next? Well, it was out of Great Keppel for us, away from the Incident, onward to Undara and some promised extraordinary geology. Ahead loomed Australia's verdant eastern Great Dividing Range—Australia's defining climate maker. We had to get past that.

I've been asked if I was ever afraid while flying, and the answer is no. However, that's so because of training. Whenever possible, my primary instructor took me out in the nastiest weather scenarios to show me how to handle them and taught me to know when *not* to go. Scud running was a no-no, but climbing through wisps to good visibility above, deviating from the course line to stay clear of obstacles, keeping aware of my position on the chart and ground, were important and useful. And so we worked ourselves around the Great Dividing Range.

A strong orographic lift condenses out copious airborne moisture blown in by prevailing winds from the eastern side of Australia, off the Pacific. Like our Rockies, but less massive and imposing, it's a cordillera that stretches north to south. It runs along the eastern/ southeastern edge of the country (and popping up again as Tasmania, after plunging down under the sea for a bit). These mountains and their varied ranges separate the enormous dry Australian western interior from the narrow eastern region. The highest point is Mount Kosciuszko at 7,310 feet. Quenching rains and dews enable good farming and excellent wineries in this relatively small part of the country.

Including the mountains themselves, the entire arable area occupies only about one-seventh of the continent. A disproportionately large amount of Australia lies west, downwind, its atmosphere wrung dry by the mountains. The land is parched and there is no chance of growing anything useful out there. The same condition exists on a smaller scale in America's western state of Washington. East of the Olympic Range around Eucla, it's pure desert in the lee of the prevailing westerlies. But in western Washington to the sea, it's so wet that tree trunks can be slippery with moss.

Like our northwest corner, mountain peaks of Australia's Great Dividing Range are often shrouded in moist clouds—and so we found them, flying along to Undara.

With a bit of careful maneuvering, we poked our way safely around and through to the beginning of an eerie dry vastness, one that reached far away to faint horizons—to the indistinct rim of what was, for us, adventure.

EN ROUTE, A TOP-OFF

Through the Rockhampton Em Bee Zed (MBZ, like our high-traffic Class B airspace) we hummed westward to refuel at the town of Charters Towers. The GPS had gotten coy. The ADF—Automatic Direction Finder—was all we had to find our way; its needle handily points directly at the transmitter. Well, the ADF was not quite all we had . . . We well-trained pilots did have a chart after all and of course knew basic pilotage. But ah! The comfort zone—Charters did indeed have an ADF beacon. Those low-frequency AM radio signals, just below the regular broadcast AM band, reach long distances. (The ADF receiver also picks up radio stations higher on the dial, nice on long, tiring flights when you might want to check the news.) But anyway, the chart showed a highway boring straight through the beige haze to Charters from the waypoint town of Emerald. No techie av crutch needed.

The town of Charters, said to be an architecturally opulent historical venue of the late 1800s and early 1900s, was not on Nick's list of must-sees for us. And its airport was desolate and desultory . . . just a fuel stop. All *we* got to see were a massive fatty's shorts.

The mountainous fueler/lineman was morbidly obese. His britches fell alarmingly short of his own rear end dividing range; his immense heft required a specially constructed steel stool. As larded as he was, and so astonishingly tall, he was nonetheless most cheerful and pleasant—if annoyingly slow moving. Well, in that heat we didn't want him to have a heart attack. Who could ever hoist him if he toppled? (One does not usually hold corpulence up for review, but that exposed backside asked for it.)

Nick laid hands on the ailing GPS and magically healed it.

"Ooh," said I, awestruck.

"Right," he smiled. "It's a gift."

On we flew, out over bewildering *terra incognita*, grateful for the GPS.

6 AUSSIE CHARTS AND RABBITS

UNDARA'S DEEP COUNTRY DIRT landing strip was located in an impressively monotonous wilderness. This was where we would discover the lava tubes.

There were few landmarks. The airstrip finally came into view after hectares upon hectares of "where are we?" forests. The strip is easier to spot today, now that it's paved. We were following charts traced with spidery roads long since overwhelmed by bushy overgrowths—bad charts, dangerous with out-of-date data and still marked long since ripped out railroad tracks. And although idiotically *not* on the chart for aerial navigation, there were plenty of good-sized airstrips, as well as in-your-face prominent landmarks—like "You Are Here" long horizon-to-horizon fences—those impressive, prominent, long-established rabbit barricades. The Australian version of our FAA, their CAA, was way behind the power curve on their charting. You must use a GPS.

One particular rabbit fence is well documented—Australia's main rabbit barrier that cordons off huge territories, one from the other. In the middle of the continent, we eventually caught sight of it.

The first fleets that sailed south to Tasmania in 1790 brought a lively food supply of domesticated European rabbits. Those not being dinner did what rabbits do, which is to procreate prolifically. In the fullness of time they made it to Australia, and then a certain fancy Thomas Austin released twenty-four wild rabbits, or hares, onto his property near Geelong, near Melbourne. These he had brought from England for some tweedy sport hunting on Christmas Day, 1859. You think they were all rounded up for the feast? Not a chance. What a ninny.

By 1886 rabbits had spread north as far as the Queensland–New South Wales border. By 1900 they had hopped, grazed, and burrowed all the way to Western Australia and the Northern Territory, becoming serious plagues and infestations to farmers and ranchers. Rabbit fencing is now one control device. And there's talk of an intentional virus to wipe them out. Some say this is good. They are incredibly destructive rodents—six small ones can strip an acre faster than one large hungry sheep—and rabbits out-populate sheep by incalculable numbers. Six hundred million dollars are spent annually on trying to control them. Species of fauna and flora like the erstwhile bilby and bandicoot are said to no longer exist because of the rabbits' relentless foraging.

En route to Undara, Nick called out prehistoric volcanic lava tube cave-ins, vaguely indicated by winding lines of heavy vegetation in low depressions, possible to pick out from our flight a few thousand feet above.

The encyclopedia tells us, "Lava tubes are natural conduits through which lava travels beneath the surface of a lava flow expelled by a volcano during an eruption. They can be actively draining lava from a source or can be extinct—the lava flow has ceased and the rock has cooled and left a long cave-like channel."

We had come for an archeological tour of this one, discovered only a few years before. Undara National Park is big—a remnant of the world's largest extinct volcano—and the runway lies on the filled-in middle of its crater. Our arrival, landing and rolling out in the middle of a big nowhere in a dry silent forest, felt most curious. Where were the birds or anything alive? Where was everybody? Where was *anybody*? Oh good. Sadie from the resort suddenly tootled out of the trees to meet us and heaved our luggage into a van. Jauntily outgoing and boyish, she had a knuckle-cracker handshake.

Australia is full of pleasant surprises. Our sleeping accommodations? We bumped along to funky and fun old railroad car bedrooms, actual antique Pullman cars, right out there in the puckerbrush.

Great gadgety idea, grabbing up old scrap train coaches to remodel for the purpose. They were quaintly comfy if not "Orient Express" elegant. Happy hour was down the path to an open-air bar, already busy with other guests, more tourists. (Undara is a national attraction—re-

A door to the bedroom.

mote, but quite a draw.) Reggie's low beer pressure light was flashing.

We grinned and goaded the bartender. "You beer-gulping Aussies don't know how to make anything but a wimpy drink." Smugly he met the challenge with a lavish orange potion poured with a flourish, knowing we could use the citrus, just the topper to a fine day and successful flight.

They were sneaky strong. So, quite unwound, we wrapped ourselves around a fire-grilled dinner of both chicken and kangaroo meat. That was memorable—but so in its own dismal way was the dessert—a tooth-breaking, unchewable, cardboard-tough apricot pie. I gummed mine a bit and then abandoned it. How did they *do* that? Aha. The sous chef was a college kid on holiday. Seems he had presented himself as a cook for a temporary job and been vague about experience. The apricots were canned anyway; no loss.

Just out of sight in the deep night beyond the campfire, a husky baritone sang to his guitar. We listened, sobered and mesmerized, to the powerful dark ballad "And the Band Played Waltzin' Matilda"—a disturbing recount of the heartrending World War I homecoming of Australian soldiers, maimed and dead. Australia, too, has played its part on the world's battlefields.

"YOU NOT RISSEN!"

Our group was quite clever. Introverted Jerry, the computer geek, turned out to have a whimsical dry wit. His occasional *bon mots* surprised us, for he otherwise was weirdly withheld. His favorite getup in the overpowering heat was a cap with neck flap à la French Foreign Legion, shirtless with boots and shorts.

At the other end of the spectrum, Reggie and Brad were hilarious cures for anything. As I said earlier, at a moment, Brad would become the slit-eyed Chinese Dr. Lie Chee or the hilarious "wobblehead" Dr. Panji-Panji telling jokes that made us gasp for breath and laugh till our eyes watered. If nothing else happened on this trip, the memory of this hilarity would be worth everything. The catchphrase became his sibilant, "Ah! You not rissen!"—a Dr. Lie Chee narrow-eyed rebuke for inattention.

Leader Nick was full of great Australian goodwill and humor. He had once worked as first officer for Ansett Australia, till he saw himself in a more interesting life in general aviation. Even now, with things gone so dreadfully awry for him, he managed to keep a good face and here and there throw us a joke. It could not have been easy, watching a chunk of his livelihood roll up into rubble on a runway. He didn't always quite know how to relate to a woman pilot with more flight hours than he had, but he kept his Aussie machismo to himself—mostly. His wife (nonpilot) had helped put together the trips, arranging the places to stay. A good team.

Snug in our cozy beds, we slept deeply in the quiet woods.

Next morning's breakfast happened at the end of a short winding stroll through dry copses to an open fire. There, guests hand toasted lovely thick bread, spreading it while hot with butter and jam. We gathered together camp-style at the fireside and drank generous cups of watery billy coffee (picturesque, but *oh* for something high impact).

Sitting on log benches, we munched scrambled eggs and crisply browned savory sausages off plates balanced on stumps. Very colorful. Our three planes were the only fly-ins; others had driven, some from far distances, to see this national geological landmark, the Undara Lava Tubes.

Vans came to gather everyone up for the tour. The guide was a lissome blonde, a scholarly ranger who knew dizzying amounts about both the tubes and the indigenous flora. Some eyes glazed over as she expounded. The tube site was quite rough and not equipped with the sort of things like accommodating steps and handrails. Scrabbling down steep rocky paths to explore the cave made my cartilage-challenged knees scream, so at the opening of the giant subterranean tube—a wide and gaping hole descending precipitously into inkiness—I simply had to stay up top to twiddle and wait.

At the base of a handsome sentinel tree I brushed off a bench-sized root to sit on. It was the granddaddy of all giant figs, with black scars of ancient campfires scorched onto its trunk. Settling myself to suffer the wilderness quite alone, I watched pensively while the group stumbled happily down into the deep, winding cavern. They finally faded off into total darkness, voices and lights slowly dimming, and then all winked out.

In the silent wilderness I waited. And waited. Uneasily. It was disturbingly remote. I was truly alone—and well, maybe there were *things* lurking. But it was so completely still my straining ears couldn't even hear a leaf rustle. I was glad.

The group's return, finally, was magical. Slowly, from the primal darkness far, far below in the yawning mouth, tiny lights floated out and upward like drifting fireflies—people moving cautiously along the path, sliding torch beams over interesting bits, lights growing in size as they quietly rose toward the surface. I wouldn't trade that sight for anything.

Undara time was up. We browsed the company store and bought mementos. A couple of kangaroos and their little joeys hopped warily through the campsite, looking for the rare patch of green grass to nibble. They were skittish, but tolerated a distant photo shoot in the cause of dinner.

Sadie gathered us up and hauled us back to our aircraft. Takeoff strategies demanded full attention, for at twenty-five hundred feet above sea level we were high, it was already hot, and after taking on fuel we were full and heavy.

Being thinner than air at sea level, hot air and high altitude are the enemies of the aerodynamics of flight. Under hot and high conditions, the number of molecules flowing over the wings to form the low pressure necessary to pull them aloft is quite reduced. The propeller also has less to bite into. So out came our pilots' operating manual, and the Koch takeoff chart graph of distance versus altitude and temperature. Calculations were made . . . And then we rolled. There was the notation to add 10 percent to the takeoff distance for grass strips. Oh boy.

First, Nick and Jerry in the Piper 140, starting back at the edge of the clearing, lumbered and strained for release from the dirt strip, finally gathering enough airspeed to heave up into "ground effect," that interesting cushion of air beneath the wings that forms at the precise distance of the wingspan length, aircraft to ground, flying parallel to the earth. It's a bit of support, space, and altitude that give a plane a chance to gather the airspeed needed for the actual climbout, without the drag of the wheels' friction rolling on the surface. Ducks and geese use this cushion while flying over water, to lighten their work. We were transfixed, giving it body English, watching the Piper slowly angle upward and claw her way aloft, finally wobbling away over the trees, brushing a few leaves with her wheels. Put the Koch chart to the test. The Cessnas had more power and less drama. Our 172 had a Penn Yan 180 horsepower conversion, extra oomph, more than the standard 150 horsepower—we fairly floated away, most grateful for our good luck at the draw of aircraft.

From there we returned eastward to cross again the Great Dividing Range. This time the weather was clear with fine visibility—no mountain mists, no scud. We flew north and east to Cooktown and the sea, to the historic and once-inhospitable landing site of the British explorer Captain James Cook. (As you probably know, Cook's prolific voyages and mappings took him around the globe, leaving little to be discovered by others. A beam of his ship *Endeavor* is on display in a museum in Rhode Island, and a nostalgic snippet of its beam went orbiting in its namesake, the Space Shuttle *Endeavor*.)

From out there on the deck, Australian *terra firma* must have looked mighty good to Cook and his crew. How could someone from mild old England suspect there'd be such harsh business ashore? (Did I mention that most everything in nature here is either caustic or poisonous?)

So at Cooktown, we would again be at sea level. No more nerve-wracking high, hot, and heavy action for a good while.

7 COOKTOWN AND LIZARD

WE WERE ALL GETTING firmly into this circumnavigation thing—hauling bags, checking charts, every couple of days digging into a new experience. But there was a problem. "Nick, I'm getting confused . . . where I've been, where I'm going, even what date it is. My circuits are overloaded!"

"That's an easy fix. Keep a diary, a log. That'll keep you on track," he responded optimistically. So I hauled out the laptop. I would download those overloaded circuits.

COOKTOWN

Cruising back over the mountains through fair skies, we flew against gentle headwinds, leaving dry, primordial Undara behind for greener territory. Making for the York Peninsula of North Queensland, steering toward the eastern horizon, we scanned ahead to find the ocean. Ah yes, there it was—its blue flatness and emerging reefs, famous waters known to cloak a startling world of darting colors—and there was the hazy shoreline just ahead. Soon, the runway.

Power back, airspeed slowly reduced for descent, we lost flying lift just as we tiptoed down on the numbers . . . perfect.

The airdrome. What's this? We had drifted into a South Sea island movie—putting-green grasses, palm trees, a caretaker's white bungalow nestled in flowering bottlebrush, banksias, and romantic swaying palms. We taxied in and stopped. Hopping out to greet the next discoveries, we felt soft breezes brush us with scent and warmth.

The Sovereign Resort Hotel rep (our hotel booking for the next two nights) came to fetch us—a big glad-handing entrepreneur with a happy red face rough and pocked with good living.

As he motored into the small town, we spied odd wen-like, man-high roadside mounds of dirt. Termites at work—an interesting departure from the pointy gothic termite structures we'd seen before. Did you know the ancient Aborigines used old abandoned mounds for ovens? The termite makes a hard, durable product. (Pretty exciting dirt-strip landing, when wham!—there they are, right on your landing spot.) Termites build everywhere, we discovered later.

Not much population out here—fifteen hundred inhabitants. With little regional traffic, only one lane was paved, "sealed," skirted with wide gravel margins for avoiding head-ons. Drivers rolled past each other in swirling dust—the "chicken" taking the gravel margin. They gestured good-natured greetings to one another, casually cocking a hand up on the steering wheel. We passed by two cars. In the gravel.

Before checking into the hotel, our man took us up to Cooktown's one major landmark to view with our own eyes, more than two centuries later, what Captain Cook had climbed up to look down upon after coming ashore in 1770. He shifted our transport's grinding gears, racketing up steep narrow switchbacks to the historic Grassy Hill outlook. There, Cook had ruefully surveyed his landing site—a very mean place back then. This day we pondered his difficulties. With breezes whispering through the grasses, it was easy to think of ghosts. Cook himself had been on this very spot, sweaty and surely rank from all that time at sea. No resort hotel for him.

Downhill we zigzagged, reversing steep horseshoe turns toward our hotel. First established in 1874, The Sovereign Resort had been always kept to the poshest standards over its long history—a boutique tropical dream of polished bare wooden floors, thick stands of bright bamboo, and elegant yet informal decor. It may have been the best lodging of our trip. A pale shimmer of blue reflected through drifting vines . . . a swimming pool beckoned from behind swaying blossoms and banana palms.

First things first. We were hungry, and that LBP light was blinking. But good grief—the dining room was not open now—it was the midafternoon hiatus.

Never mind. Here was our chance to catch the lay of the land. Hotel staff directed us to a bistro/sandwich shop at the corner, a short walk to late lunch. Inside with the air conditioning sat full-blooded, dark Aborigines—pouchy cheeks, large black eyes overhung by thick shelflike brows—the main characteristics of faces that have developed over millennia, features to accommodate and protect from the fierce sunlight. Since the gene pool has been fermenting for more than sixty thousand years, it was no surprise.

Anyway, they weren't there for the food—they were drinking up their government checks. The uninvited appearance and influx of radically different Europeans to their land was not a happy thing for the natives; first the Europeans took their land away and then would-be do-gooders, appalled and totally ignorant of these people, initially took their children away from them to raise them the European way—a dreadful and devastating practice. This horror eventually stopped, and the Australian government came to pay the Aborigine a stipend, supposed to help "bring them along." (Conscience money?) But as with the Amerind and Inuit, irresistible firewater was a genetic problem, and mostly the check was pissed out into the dirt.

The afternoon drifted by; the sun remained blindingly hot. After lunch, we moved sluggishly back to the shade-dappled pool for a revitalizing paddle-about surrounded by the tropical garden and then to our rooms to stretch out. In the evening, dinner called from the deep veranda, with candlelit white tablecloths and gleaming wood floors, *al fresco*. The day's heat had lifted; evening was cool bliss.

In the morning, a reef trip in a glass-bottomed boat had been on the docket, but as long-distance arrangements sometimes don't firm up, this one awkwardly had not. What would Nick do with us? He had some mechanical issues to take care of at the airdrome—a faulty vacuum pump, the inevitable sorting out of the Incident . . . There were numerous arrangements and phone calls to occupy him. So despite dire misgivings about letting us fly off on our own, he now considered it. We had, of course, studied our charts. We hungered for so much more than some glass-bottomed boat.

Palpitating over the nearness of famous Lizard Island and the Great Barrier Reef, locus of arguably the earth's most colorful corals and exotic tropical fish, we now pushed for it. All of us pilots were of one mind. So, poor Nick, distraught from Keppel's events, gave in and gave us a worried go-ahead. To top it all off, he was festering a zinger of a sore throat and nasty cold. "Ah, no dramas . . . it'll be all right." Reggie rummaged about in his bag of pharmaceuticals and pulled out some emergency antibiotics, muttering, "But all you need to do, actually, is drink it away, Nick. Alcohol will kill it." With a headshake, Nick accepted the pills.

LIZARD . . . THE GREAT BARRIER REEF

We had hopelessly lusted to bob and snorkel about over the famed Great Barrier Reef. Reggie had tormented us with his wild and windy tale of flying over to Tasmania, a very big deal—and all *we* wanted to do was take a tame short zip over to Lizard. It had not been on offer. But now, a hop over to our dreams—on our own! Out came the charts and pencils to draw lines away out over the water. The hotel loaded us up with a picnic hamper and off we went with agonized admonitions from poor beleaguered Nick. Happy? We were like bounding dogs escaping through an unhooked gate.

Lizard Island, a resort renowned world round for wondrous varieties of reef life, had a one hundred dollar landing fee per plane to keep out the crowds—the hotel, nine hundred dollars per room per night. The toll taker emerged from his shed, beady-eyeing us pleasantly. We gratefully paid the beach-only landing fee, with snorkeling privileges. Good enough.

It was Hal's birthday, and so his birthday flight. (A gift of love. To make things fair and peaceful, we usually alternated legs, and it was supposed to be my turn.) With eagerness salted with bravado we assumed our roles to find our way—he pilot, I navigator. Scrupulously sticking to the straight line, no ducking off course for look-sees, out of Cooktown we aimed north up the coastline—and angled away from continental Australia. As the shore disappeared behind us, we bored anxiously through the sea haze trying to spy land again and destination Lizard Island. No dramas . . . it showed up soon, right out there on the nose. (I think it took three minutes . . . well, maybe fifteen.)

Landing was easy and routine, a paved runway like any other. What did we expect? Later in the trip we would find dirt strips erupting with challenging termite mounds—but we didn't know about those yet. The overhill trail to the beach was taxing. We panted and hiked and kvetched . . . Were we on the right path? Should we have gone left back there? The lunch cooler was heavy and got heavier . . . After a sweaty hike and a half up the hill, we passed the crest. Downhill below stretched a perfect white crescent beach, some sails lightly billowing on a boat lying to in the bay. And lookee there . . . a seaplane in the lagoon's serene waters, the Southern Cross painted on its tail. A clever fellow had sidestepped the landing fee—and the hike—by not using the airstrip.

Staggering downhill, picnic hamper in tow, we merrily flung our towels out wide and flopped down to rest, and then we rocketed up howling in stinging pain, flailing arms and legs, kicking up sand. We had landed in the Lizard Island version of fire ants—like hitting live wires. What a horrible beginning.

Singularly unimpressed by the trailside scenery, Brad and Reggie just had to show off. They had disappeared on a brisk scramble up to the island's highest point. Like whooping schoolboys they returned bragging about seeing a fearful giant goanna—the famous large debatably venomous lizard, a type of monitor—and laughing at us as we thrashed our way out of the ant attack. Oh good for them. We didn't need to see any giant lizard. Sour grapes? You bet. Fie on their gloating eyes.

We dove into the hamper and feasted on elegant hotel sandwiches, fruit tarts, coffee, and bottled water. Well away from any ants. Appetites satisfied, strength restored after the overhill hike, we rigged up with masks and breathing tubes and then snorkeled till we turned blue and beyond. The beauty of the reef was more breathtaking than ever seen in *National Geographic*.

Besides the drifting, startlingly vibrant, wildly exotic fish and swaying coral life, behind those waving veils of darting fins and see-through fan corals, it turned out that our particular reef ridge was actually a mammoth colony *of sea clams*. As we scrutinized our venue closely through the magnifying glass of the masks, we discovered a fanciful collection of every shape, color, and size of clam imaginable, all neatly fitted and wedged together. From giant to tiny, from great pulsing velvety neon-spotted lips to little wee zipper-like slits—their crescent shells were astonishingly rimmed with shimmering beads of cobalt blue, or electric orange, or some of the brightest green—all fluorescing in the filtered sunlight. Gorgeous colors, caused entirely by algae. The variety of all aspects of these bivalves was extraordinary. Some were as tiny as dimes, and at least one was about the size of a king-sized bed. I wondered seriously if I would fit into that big one if he decided he wanted more than plankton . . .

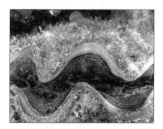 

While drifting facedown in the gentle tide aimlessly scrutinizing this display, all of a sudden, in one terrifying, paralyzing moment, my eyes fell on . . . *what was this*! A single large golden goatish eye—surveying *me*. A god-awful enormous octopus had locked its gaze on mine from his hidden viewing post in the reef—like maybe I could be dinner? They weren't visible, that vicious parrot-like octopus beak mouth and those long suction-cup-lined tentacles. But of course they were there all right, down in that hidey-hole right along with the rest of him. Jesus, Mary, and Joseph, might it snap-wrap me with its eight arms (tucked away now, but could be whipped out in a flash) and dissect me as easily as ripping up a shrimp? Would I be efficiently shredded while drowning? They say octopuses feed at night, but maybe this one didn't know that. All were thoughts of a nanosecond. Applying high octane to my flippers, I rocketed away, racking up amazing cramps in every leg muscle. My feet got so rigidly locked up, once back safely on the sand I couldn't even get the swim fins off. But what an incredible, unforgettable sight. A fine swap for the glass-bottomed boat.

The reef visit done, flying back was bewitching. The sun's rays were at a low angle, modeling the hilly shoreline and highlighting occasional sheer luminescent wisps of cloud, the clouds drifting above a varicolored, shimmering sea, forming moving rainbows. And so we returned to Cooktown. Nick was there to greet and fetch us, grinning and elated that we hadn't killed ourselves.

Our sunburns were impressive, and we were exhausted. It was so worth it. Hal found some helpful aloe to slather, all night long. But no sunburn was going to upstage our five-star dinner, whipped up by the Sovereign's own five-star French chef. His *chef d'oeuvre* was Hal's birthday cake, a great rich chocolate nut creation, served with celebratory champagne. What could top this? Brad thought maybe the cute Danish waitress.

That was not in the cards.

8 BURKETOWN . . .

OR FROM YIN TO YANG

Fresh soft breezes drifted through breakfast on the deck. Bills settled up, baggage in the van, Brad´s Danish waitress sought out and wistfully adieu'd— we headed through the sunshine to gas up the planes, a process done from a fuel drum on the back of a pickup truck. This was hardly standard operating procedure in the United States, but commonplace here. We

Rainbow Lorakeet at breakfast

topped off for a long flight against forecasted headwinds, the gas laboriously and patiently hand pumped up into the wing tanks.

Departing the Cooktown airdrome, pilots took up a slightly zigzag track for sightseeing, first taking a south-westerly heading of 210 degrees and then shifting course at Wrotham Park to 242 and at Normanton to 261.

We passed over long hectares of, well, at first not much. Peering down, we saw thinly treed territories of swelling hills slowly transition into vast arid areas of khaki-colored flat clay pans—those smooth, dried-out leftovers from wet season pools—and the odd parched braided river. Here and there a twisting dry bed was sunlit, gleaming, silver streaked with shining water—the "Waltzin' Matilda" billa-bong (lyrics in appendix), where the jolly swagman (itiner-ant worker carrying his swag or bedroll) set up camp and boiled his billy, or teapot. And looking closer, we spied relic mines left from old-time gold rush days (Aussies are nick-named "diggers").

Well, no headwinds after all; the circuitous flight of 660 km took little more than three and a half hours, burning 10.4 gallons per hour, 36.4 gallons used out of the more than 50 in the tanks. So the extra fuel wasn't necessary, but who knew?

OLD PILOT SAYINGS:

"The three most useless things in the world—gas in the truck, runway behind you, and altitude above you." It can be a bad decision to take on only what the leg requires. Always best to fuel up for as much as your weight and balance allow, start at the very beginning of the runway for takeoff, and maximize your gliding distance in case of engine failure—don't risk a sad landing out with engine trouble (glide range is in the pilot's operating manual). That last one is hard to obey, because sometimes the low-level sightseeing is worth the risk. You have to weigh the pros and cons.

Nearing Burketown, a settlement in a far-off, very lonely area of Australia (there are reasons), we strayed over to the lapping edge of the Gulf of Carpentaria to check for lazing crocodiles. The sweeping saline flats are home to a large population of the armor-skinned creatures, once shot for designer-chic shoes and bags. We scanned the scored, ridged limestone leading from the surf back to thick interwoven mangroves, flying no lower than three hundred feet to avoid bird strikes—but no, no crocs. The day's heat had already fired up and soared—it was way past the postdawn warm-up hour that they need. They evidently had lumbered back into the shade. Unarable, inhospitable, harsh, and unpretty, this beachless coast. Not pretty, but intriguing, with huge stretches of long striations of deeply gouged coastal limestone. Curious scars from heavy ancient beasts clawing up to feed? Or *whooff!* Maybe even Neptune's angry probing trident? Well, why not? It's a wonderfully weird land.

It was technically a clear-sky approach to our landing site, but Burketown, twenty miles inland from the coast, was hard to find in the dust-polluted air. It slowly emerged vaguely through a thick beige haze. There was no hint of moisture, therefore no possibility of our catching the ephemeral Burketown phenomenon, the famous Morning Glory cloud. The glider magnet. Yes, bleak and dilapidated old Burketown offered more than history.

THE MORNING GLORY CLOUD

A spectacular and unique phenomenon occasionally swirls over Burketown. If you're lucky, you get to see it. A six-hundred-mile-long oddly tubular cloud formation rolls out at certain times of the year from opposing air masses colliding over the York Peninsula. The masses move in toward each other from the Sea of Carpentaria to the west and, from the other way, to the opposing Pacific to the east. Having formed this amazing long, ropelike streamer cloud, this meteorological anomaly streaks westward at dawn and beyond, barreling over the town parallel to the ground at thirty-five miles an hour, at anywhere from five hundred to one thousand feet overhead. It spins and rolls backward— opposite its forward progress—stirring up a mighty internal wind but leaving behind a dead calm after its passage, an

An oddity: multiple morning glories

event that takes only a few minutes. Glider pilots and cloud buffs come fervently praying to find it, for besides being quite exciting to see, it makes for excellent long soaring glider flights as long as you stay at its leading edge. The backside will drop you like a set of car keys into the no-man's distant land of risky landing "out"—the place of no airports. The cloud is a rare, shall we say, pictograph of the usually invisible location of strong rising air or "lift," the sought-after treasure of these pilots, the raison d'etre of the sailplane—nature's engine that hoists them aloft.

ABOUT GLIDERS

Gliders have a much lower structural never-exceed speed than sturdier power planes—go too fast and they can break apart. They're strongly but lightly constructed to be as close to air's weight as possible for their necessarily slow maneuverings—slower because of their extra-long wings for extra-good lift. Therefore, towing them aloft requires adrenaline-stirring slow flight by the powered plane, flight on the edge of its stall—a stall is the speed at which the shudder and flop happens when the plane runs out of enough airspeed to maintain lift for flight.

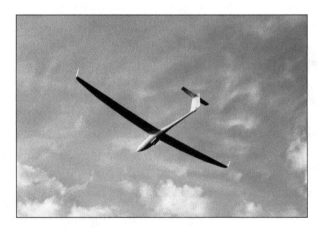

As a tow pilot I had enjoyed hauling those long-winged craft up to a useful altitude, the altitude for a safe glide, while at the same time probing air currents for strong thermal lift to release them in, the good updraft that provides the glider pilot's goal . . . good soaring. We always scanned the skies for clues, looking for circling hawks to join and concave-based cumulus clouds, signs of rising air currents—though there are also "blue thermals" found only by the bump of an updraft.

The most pleasure I got from towing was rescuing gliders from off-airport landing sites. As the day goes by the sun heats the land less, and those treasured thermals fade and die. Sometimes a pilot is so besotted with his happy cloud-hopping and yo-yoing successfully across the countryside, he loses track of time and place. The inevitable "uh–oh" invades his bliss, and he casts frantically about for a safe flat place to set down. The best of course is home base, but by now he is beyond gliding distance. Another airport is next best. He prefers to land where the tow plane can come get him, rather than a farmer's field where he must disassemble the sailplane to trailer it back to base. There's generally someone to call for help. It's a sociable sport.

MY FAVORITE RESCUE

One day I answered a late afternoon call from one who had "landed out." The thing was, his chosen flat spot was a new inter-state highway construction site . . . on a very small bit of it, a just-completed paved overpass. The roadway itself was still in process with roughed-out road approaches on either side. His glider was situated at one end of the paved piece. Touching down just past him, I rolled out and braked to a halt at the far end of this short section, stopping just in time to keep from toppling off into rocks and ruin. I gunned the engine to turn around and taxied back to him. We surveyed the job to be done and paced off the takeoff distance. It was doable. I hooked up my tail tow rope to the glider's nose ring—there's a rope release inside the cockpit for the pilot to pull, allowing the glider to veer away into its free flight. Rolling forward I gently pulled the towrope tight. Tail waggles given signaling for the "go," I slowly moved forward, gathering speed, flaps extended for extra lift to quickly get up into ground effect, at around forty-five miles per hour. He followed suit at the end of the tightened rope. There was a giddy moment at the catastrophic drop-off—but we were already up and flying. The suspense was intense. We had seen the reality of those grim piles of rocks and dirt. Ah—we knew we could make it.

THAT TOW PLANE

This happened just as I will tell you, and I will go to my grave knowing its truth.

Generally, people believe airplanes are simply clever engineering arrangements of rivets, sheets of metal, and strategically connected cables. But I know better. They are far more than that. They are magic . . . absolute magic. You form a relationship with your aircraft. Treat it right, and it will treat you right. It will tell you things about itself by whispering engine sounds only you can sense, sounds that make you rush it to the mechanic and tell him about it—and he finds a telltale bunch of iron shreds in the oil pan. Things like that. Or more radically—well, I'll tell you a tale.

My glider club had moved to an airfield rather far from our home, and I became less involved in its operations. But I still felt a closeness to that tail dragger Bird Dog tow plane, C305A, a single-engine Cessna that had been a reconnaissance plane during World War II. I had logged over two hundred hours flying her and over one thousand towing operations. That bird and I had a good relationship and I missed her. Anyway . . . One evening I took the boys flying—one was going to visit a friend and the other came along for the ride. As I taxied our plane toward the runway in the darkening twilight, out of the corner of my eye I seemed to catch a glimpse of that Bird Dog parked in a line of other aircraft, and I wondered about that. What would she be doing here? But I dismissed it—maybe just my imagination?

Mission accomplished, we were back at home base having bedded down our aircraft. We got in the car, started up to drive away, and suddenly a voice in my head, clear as a bell, insistently announced, "Come see about me . . . Come see about me!"

I turned to my younger son and said, "Whoa, we have to check on something. Hang on." I rotated the car on the grass where we were parked, headed back across to the other tie downs, and behold . . . there she was. It was by then quite dark, so I shone the headlights on her. She seemed okay from the back. But I got out, walked around her, and holy God, the poor thing had a wretchedly curled propeller! Who had done this sad damage? That, she didn't tell me. But, by heavens, she wanted me to know about it. I later found out another tow pilot had not handled the controls well while taxiing in the wind, allowing her to pitch forward onto her nose—and so he wrecked her. Sudden engine stop, the whole mess.

Airplanes are magic. Believe it.

BURKETOWN LANDING

So, here in Burketown we came down through the Australian heat and carefully touched down, an extended final over the runway in the hot air, rising currents of air off the blacktop keeping us afloat. We glanced around. No gliders in sight. The airstrip seemed higher than the rest of the area, and so it was, being located strategically to be out of the regional floodwaters during the Wet. For three whole months Burketown is absolutely, totally, marooned. It looked as remote as Mars.

We were exceedingly thirsty, but first things first—offloading morning coffee. Rushing across the baking ramp to the water closet, I swung open the door, and gave a startled eek and jump . . . a little frog lurking in the privy—the beastie's only water source during the Dry. It was not about to move. Well, so be it. Flushing done, unperturbed froggy tucked under the rim, we slatted about trying to locate transport. Wasn't someone supposed to pick us up?

Where was our ride? The phone at our lodgings was busy . . . busy . . . busy. Nick could not get through. Embarrassing. Eventually, a couple of us convinced the fueler to take us into town, a stark little settlement of only 180 or so people. That ride was awkward, the driver silent and surly. Reggie said he must have been dragged away from the bar to work the gas pumps.

Rolling up to the inn just behind its pub, we found the door bolted. How special. Nobody to greet or take us from the airport, the manager unreachable by phone, and now a locked door.

We ambled around to the pub entrance—a down-and-dirty dive with serious color. No manager there, so we settled in for a chilled VB (Victoria Bitter beer). It felt mighty good, washing down our dry throats. Air conditioning blew cool relief on our sweat. Friendly nods from locals at our elbows perked us up—but they were a whiffy lot—sunburned and rank, wanting a good scrub. To go with the scruffy clientele, the walls and ceiling were covered, corner to corner, with years of salty writing of those who had passed through from far, far away.

Burketown bar

Pleasingly funky. Otherwise—a pit.

Look at that—the bar phone was off the hook. Brilliant. No wonder Nick couldn't raise a ride. The manager finally surfaced. He was absolutely huge. Howard the Huge—tall, rotund, pale, and fleshy—and new to the job. He announced ambitious plans to "get rid of all that ugly scribbling and clean it up good with nice white paint and pale blue trim. That'll bring some respect in here." No! No! No! Don't wipe out those happy beery messages. Please. It has cachet, a fun rowdy read. It goes with the neighborhood! Nope. He knew his mind.

So Howard and Reggie set off for the airport to retrieve the others, leaving me alone with my VB—and the characters. They gripped their bee-ahs, eyeing me sidelong. Uh-oh . . . Dealing with these barflies might get tricky. I turned to the barmaid to chat her up. Pretty young Simona turned out to be from Holland. The Dutch have had a longtime association with Australia.

Simona was good for a distracting conversation, but I was relieved when Hal and our crew showed up. Brad grabbed a VB, raised a toast with the aromatic "Horny Old Goat" (the label on the geezer's cap), and it got real sociable. Oh, but our sightseeing tour was waiting.

Howard heaved his mass into a seasoned Land Cruiser, rocking it on its frame, to haul us around town and into the "flats"—the pancake-flat area surrounding all of Burketown. Flooding during the Wet quite irons out the acreage.

THE HISTORY

First, a look at the famed Landsborough Tree, getting out to attempt to decipher its unreadable sun-bleached sign. This tree was the desolate appointed meeting place where explorers Burke and Wills fatefully missed each other literally by hours. (Explorer Landsborough, sent to search for Burke and Wills, is a big part of Australian history himself.)

We tooled on down to the Albert River Bridge on the croc-infested waterway. I moved to go closer, which brought a bellow and harsh lecture out of Nick—just last year a youngster was grabbed and pulled under by a slithering crocodile—the tragic, grisly end of that boy. Crocs pull you under to drown you and then store you till you've rotted to an edible consistency. Such an appetizing thought.

The van crawled along its tourist route. There was the ugly but interesting Burketown natural geothermal bore—a small hot spring gently erupting curbside, coated with scuzzy crusty layers of minerals, an ancient bore burbling hot water. We then drifted past the old cemetery, the new little school, the nurses' clinic, and the little library. Yep. This also was Australia, rustic and rudimentary—with history.

Farther out of town, we meandered onto scorched expanses of smooth hardened dirt, the hot, depressing flats—to view the defunct Old Meat Works, aka the Boiler Factory. Here, cattle had been rendered and processed for large markets like Sydney. Its remains were now a discouraging scatter of rusted debris toasting in the searing sun and dirt—unsightly debris of the past. We were seeing the seamy side of Australia, not just the lovely. It marked a significant part of its past.

There outside of town Howard got himself quite turned around. Disoriented. Lost. He nervously picked up speed with each circling about, following *this* set of looping tire tracks and then *that* set (there was a confusing profusion)—rattling madly along on bewildering paths that fed back on themselves.

LOST AMONG COW CAKES

He was indeed *very* lost, and we got to snickering. No definitive landmarks . . . nothing there except for the odd bush and mind-numbing number of dried cow puckies, the locale's dominant *je ne sais quoi*. We were round-eyed at his fruitless circle-backs, occasionally passing boiler factory detritus again, exciting us with a momentary frisson of hope—when suddenly, at last, he spied the microwave tower, Burketown's connection to the world, and homed in on it. "I was not lost," he scowled. Vehemently, "I was not!"

Oh yeah? Personally, I had begun to have unpleasant death-in-the-desert thoughts, fingering my water bottle . . .

I asked him if during the three wet months of being marooned together (heavy persistent rains do indeed isolate the area) the 180 Burketown residents didn't get on each other's nerves, all cooped up like that, and somebody want to kill somebody. He muttered that they were already on each other's nerves.

Burketown had another point of interest. It was said to be the barramundi fishing capital of Australia and site of seasonal competitions. So, when dinnertime came, our mouths were watering expectantly. But no, just beef. Humph. Standard operating procedure: order dinner at the bar, exit to the back, and feed at picnic tables. The steaks were delicious actually, and since I wasn't so gung ho for fish, I was fine with that. But Nick had been going on so about barramundi.

After dinner, Reggie and Brad, looking for a more excitement than the flats and the thermal bore, trotted off into the darkening dust. The local Rodeo Bar roadhouse held beery promises. The rest of us turned in shortly—the morning's plan was to get out early.

9 BORROLOOLA TO GOVE/ NHULUNBUY

HAVING SO VERY WISELY bedded down early (what else?) to get a good start onward to Nhulunbuy at the Gove Peninsula, we were up at dawn, impatient to see the last of Burketown.

Bad idea. Turned the faucet handle. No water. Not a drip or dribble. So, no showers, brushing teeth, flushing, anything. We emerged to see if anyone else was stirring. Nope. No cook, no coffee. That was the worst of it. That made us ponder our Aussie lads' condition . . . They had frolicked off into the dark the night before. They hadn't surfaced. Did they get back? We slumped about, irritated.

No sense spinning wheels. Just be patient, we advised ourselves. Sure enough, after a bit the water kicked in, the cook showed up, and so did the guys. Ah, but they were slow and dull from their stint at the Rodeo Bar, yee-haw. They'd better get better—there's a legal limit of eight hours, bottle to throttle, to act as pilot in command. But the foggy cook didn't organize himself exactly chop-chop; the kitchen was unhurried, cranking itself up to speed. So the required time lapse for the regulations on alcohol was fulfilled, and everybody seemed fitter after a good breakfast. The men's recovery rate was astonishing.

Across the way, a grizzled old Aborigine sat stiffly on a park bench. He hadn't moved for the longest time, rigid as a board. Had he been there like that all night? Could he be, God help him, dead? So pitifully out of the modern mainstream they hurt your sensibilities, drooping about, drunk, government support checks enabling their addiction. Sadly, the Aborigines seemed a lost species.

To be fair, they didn't invite Europeans to come aboard—and before they did come, the Aborigines had their own successful way of living, one that had worked very well for at least forty thousand years. For the survival of their prehistoric culture, there are some remote communities where alcohol is forbidden, where they can by choice keep to their ancient ways. And then again, some have adapted well to Western civilization; TV spokesmen, tennis pros, and so on. But they can look different from anyone else in the world. By Western standards, often they seem quite homely. And then again, some are strikingly handsome. They drift slowly through the heat in small groups, some with large bushy heads over huge eyes, wide mouths, and big teeth and some with incredibly tall thin bodies. Legs attached to impossibly narrow hips. Stick figures. It's said that given a reason, they can run like gazelles. They once believed storms impregnated, so when a rain cell appeared on the horizon they would streak off alarmed in the opposite direction. Whenever we saw them, they were just sitting in groups in the shade—drinking, talking, watching.

Hal drily remarked that in the United States, once upon a time, a cop would have motioned them along saying, "You there, move along now. No loitering here, you know."

Interesting, the government-supported life of this tiny historical outpost. Otherwise just a sad, drunken dump.

Well, there is the Morning Glory cloud . . . If you can get lucky.

We didn't.

THE DOVE

At the airport, a big de Havilland Dove, a charter plane, stood at the bowser. A popular plane back in 1941; at more than half a century old, it had logged only fourteen hundred hours. (Airplanes measure age by hours flown, not so much by years or flight miles covered.) The pilots, who swore that the Dove was the last of its model off the line, had a glider business also. Remember that coveted Morning Glory cloud. An amazing phenomenon, but so unpredictable.

We loaded up, did our preflights, cleared the propeller by calling out "clear prop" to the world outside the cockpit, and looked about carefully to see if anyone was out front in the way. All being safe and clear, we fired up.

The engine caught, shuddered dramatically, and then abruptly stopped. The silence was intense. Whatever could be wrong? Please, oh please, no troubles.

Here we were in the middle of nothing and nowhere. Not a maintenance shop for hundreds of miles. "Houston, we have a problem." Could our engine have gone bad? At least we were still on the ground.

Smarting mortification. In very carefully concentrating

on accommodating the scorching heat, Hal had leaned the mixture of air to fuel to provide less fuel for the extremely warm air. But he had overleaned it—which accidentally starved the start-up, choking it right off, with a conspicuous shudder and stop. Just the way you shut down the engine at the end of the flight. It might have been my fault—I had stressed leaning the mixture for hot weather start-up. The cockpit air turned righteous blue. Never mind. He recovered, judiciously increased the gas, fired her up, and radioed his departure intentions. I imagined snickers from our pals. It's amateurish to overlean, and they were merciless.

It was Hal's flight to the Borroloola fuel stop, en route to Nhulunbuy (discombobulating names that point out again that you're far from home). It was nice to be up into a cooler atmosphere. On the air-to-air frequency, Nick pointed out termite mounds, each standing in the middle of its own round bare area . . . trampled clear by cattle having a rump scratch. What sights . . . Impressionist pastels of silvery eucalyptus brushed on terra cotta earth, distant rosy hills tracing a horizon nearly lost in hazy smoke from Aboriginal agricultural burning. They've been managing the land properly for thousands and thousands of years . . . eons that brought them the know-how.

Descent into Borroloola slid us back into the oven—one hundred degrees in the shade. The pilot of a local plane marked ShawFlight ambled out to greet us, asking how long we were staying in "The Loo," the small town's cynical sobriquet. "There's a stereo in that Cessna 210," he said, pointing proudly to his charter plane. Good for long flights over the outback—both the 210 and its stereo.

It was noon, time to scout out lunch. The airfield

abutted the settlement—only a short block into its center. Sweat running into our eyes, we punched through the heat under trees noisy with flitting parrots, a brief walk to the Everything Store for savory hot sausage rolls. Time was important that day—so just a quick snack, for Nhulunbuy, the day's destination, was still many miles away. This store was as close to fast food as it got, and as Nick had promised, it was indeed good. We never had problems with food anywhere in Australia. (Well, except Undara's Apricot Toughie.) Grilled at the counter, those sausage sandwiches were delicious.

Besides those surprising, mouthwatering sandwiches, the well-named Everything Store was stocked with a potpourri of everything else . . . from Levis, plastic storage containers, machine oil, bread, and milk, to paper towels, batteries, shovels—and wow—tall Hal spied the top shelf's supply of lice shampoo. Ugh. Lice apparently were so prevalent they even sold treatments here at the convenience store. Our scalps started to itch.

Outside, we stepped around an out-cold form sprawled across the path. Hard life. The town was so ratty, rundown, and remote. But for us, a most critical fuel stop. They were few and very far apart out here. And so we got another angle on Australia, a take on more of the hot, seamy parts. To get from one coast to the other, we had to frolic through it.

It was a quick reversal back to the airport, passing again below the raucous parrots to preflights in the scorching sun—and the inevitable hot and heavy liftoff. This time, it was my turn. At least I didn't have to stagger up and out over obstacles—Borroloola had good approaches.

Established in a climb, I banked toward distant Gove,

once a Royal Australian Air Force field during World War II, on the Gove Peninsula, now known as Nhulunbuy's regional airport. At Gove we would tie down and then go around by car to bunk in Nhulunbuy for the night. Nick's son would be there.

Climbing to sixty-five hundred feet we found a smooth ride and the relief of cooler upper air (sixty degrees Fahrenheit), better groundspeed, and a *sensational* view. The Gulf's coastal plains were back in sight, striated sandstone pierced here and there by ornate river deltas and shifting shades of aqua. It was romantic, a landscape brushed with sea mist. A particularly large delta passed below—Blue Mud Bay, cobalt dashed with rhythmic curves of silvery sandbars. We noted that there were again several uncharted airports. Super landmarks, if only we had known what they were. We dodged east, bypassing the Roper River checkpoint, short-cutting over Groote Eylandt (there's that Dutch . . . almost English, no?) to shorten flying time and limit fuel burn. Besides the issue of endurance, at four dollars a gallon, fuel was costly. Unfortunately, our plane's 180 horsepower conversion was placarded against continuous operations between 2150 and 2350 rpms to avoid destructive engine harmonics. No economy cruise settings for us. More of an issue for Nick—the tour's price included fuel.

TESTY TOWER

I announced to area aircraft, "All stations Gove, ("stations" means other aircraft) Sierra Charlie Uniform (SCU, our aircraft identification), twenty miles to the west, estimating Gove in fifteen minutes." Now to call the tower.

In listening to their automated information, we noted that Gove had a frequency change NOTAM (Notice to Airmen), a service required by ICAO (International Civil Aviation Organization), the organization that rules aviation worldwide. The NOTAM date stated "effective 10-7," which would be October 7, and we were now in September. But since the Australians do day first and then month, that could be July 10. What a conundrum. What to do, what to do?

Here we were in September, believing that *of course* the frequency at the Australian airport had changed back in July, since they do things their way. Are you befuddled? We sure were. Turned out they went by our book on this one. They were still using the old frequency, waiting for October. Some of us were flummoxed enough to take no chances and used all frequencies available, just in case. That worked. Of course the tower was a little testy, being the tower.

Overlooking the York Peninsula as we approached the airdrome, what arose to our astonished eyes was a remarkable, wide flat landscape of intense vermilion—a vivid red bauxite mine just to the east had changed the region into something surreal. And tracing a black line geometrically straight across, a huge conveyor belt was rumbling raw material for several kilometers to the harbor for export. What a wondrous sight, the grand sweep of saturated red earth juxtaposed against the luminous blue sea. It was an abstract painting, a Paul Klee . . . fabulous.

During certain months, fires nibble away at the bush from eons-old Aboriginal practices of burn-clearing. The area forecast predicted occasional low visibility in smoke. Sure enough, we flew the normal rectangular landing pattern (left turns, downwind, base leg, and then final approach) and found half of Gove's airstrip IMC (instrument meteorological conditions) in a mile-wide plume of thick smoke crossing from adjacent fields. No worries, mate. The touchdown zone was VMC (Visual Meteorological Conditions – shorthand for being able to see where you're going). Just land in the clear, roll out, stop in the smoke, reverse direction, and cautiously grope/taxi back to clear air. Normal.

While lugging bags across the ramp, we skidded and slithered on jillions of round red bauxite beads underfoot. I grabbed some up for back home show-and-tell.

But strange how up close they lost their life, their vibrancy—like looking at a Seurat pointillist painting too close up.

We were now at the northernmost point of our travels, but not yet halfway.

NHULUMBUY and the AUSTRALIAN RULES

Nick's grown son Mark, a lad from a first marriage, worked at the Gove airdrome. Nick had commandeered him to transport us to dinner and beds in nearby Nhulunbuy. But before anything else, Mark off-loaded a heavy bag of his mechanical stuff from our plane's cargo (which subsequently improved SCU's performance). Nice fellow—like his father. After hotel check-in, we headed to a private club where locals ate, gambled, played pool, and so on. Non-Aborigine. And this was where we finally sampled the highly touted Australian freshwater barramundi. A little

like sea bass, but better. We agreed it was worth its reputation . . . but perhaps preparation is everything.

Here we had our first up-close view of an Aboriginal Caucasian mix. A cute little girl frolicked around the
pool tables, skin the color of dark honey, big brown eyes,
café-au-lait-colored curly hair. When the black Aborigine
mates with a white, black is recessive. Within six genera-
tions, Aboriginal characteristics are gone. Interesting. The
strawberry-blonde young mother was there, the white part
of the equation, and latched onto us till we went to dinner.
She was so sweet and wine friendly, but so clingy, that when
she asked for our US phone number, I deviously gave her
our fax number. No way was I going to spin out the relationship. One of our guys said, "No worries, you are not
responsible even if you feel that way." Later, back home, I
felt awful when the fax number rang, many times, over the
first month of our return.

Having tucked ourselves into dinner (from the quirky
Aussie word "tucker" for food) and brushed off our laps, we
wandered through a darkened park toward distant lights
and riotous sounds of cheering. A crowd had gathered
around a "playing oval" (ball field) to watch a game of
Australian Rules—a type of football. Most players, and the
crowd, were Aborigines. And most were beer packing and
polluted. Men freely whizzed wherever; an old man in a
wheelchair guzzled his beer and let go where he sat, leaking
a stream out below him. We considered our shoes and what
we might have been stepping in, there in the dark.

4X BEER

Far northern Queensland was fondly known as F-N-Q, eff-en Q, FNQ. The territory was mostly inhabited by Aborigines. "F-N (effin') Queensland," Brad said. At that time there was a move to give FNQ an Aboriginal name with much dithering over the choice. There were so many dialects it was said they couldn't find a single word or phrase in common. Reggie snorted and said it should be named 4X, "XXXX"—their favorite beer and a wry critique of the regional literacy and culture.

Raising our eyes to the stars, away from the *de facto* outdoor pee potty, we saw a startlingly brilliant crescent moon. It was like an eerie slice of psychedelic melon against the black sky, so perfectly balanced it seemed at rest on an invisible table, afloat in space. And no air traffic.

Thinking again of our shoes, we didn't linger. Back at our room, the TV had a *précis* of Diana's funeral. We thought about that, too.

A note from management on our door stated the hotel's electricity would be shut off at eight in the morning, for the day, for unexplained reasons. We sank into sleep, vowing to be in time for the gas-grilled breakfast. Well, we at least got a grilled croissant but missed the critical coffee. Brad and I tried to hammer our way into the dispensing machine, but sadly, no joy. It was built like a bank vault.

Some mornings are like that.

ON TO KAKADU PARK, COOINDA

After Mark off-loaded that heavy tool bag, SCU's performance got significantly livelier.

Once in the past I had to fly an aircraft where a passenger placed his hefty case in the cargo, and I had the devil of a time with directional control. It turned out the bag contained a large, functioning gyroscope—it of course interfered with controlling the aircraft. When we got to our destination, the bag itself demonstrated how it didn't like to be moved, having its own mind, and leaned this way and that as we hoisted it. Though stowed all the way in the back, it had insistently, and unnervingly, fought the plane's movements.

We now climbed quickly to eighty-five hundred feet to try to get above the murk, but that wasn't high enough. Never mind—we found excellent ground speeds and a cool outside air temperature, and though quite hazy, the views continued to be spectacular. Our track would take us west to Maningrida and then a jog southwest to Jabiru and then over the mountains and into Cooinda, the town of our destination—locus of the amazing Kakadu National Park. Gagudju is how the Aborigine says it.

We drifted past Arnhem Bay and Buckingham Bay, following the coast along the Arafura Sea with waters of sparkling brilliant aqua. An occasional sculpture of red sandbar spun sensuously out though the waters . . . The coastline was always astonishingly beautiful—and completely uninhabited and inhospitable. Long scraped stony flats stretched to the coastline, plunging into sand and wild thick brackens of shore mangroves. Marvelous textures. Said to be full of crocs. Hal was piloting, pointing out sinuous coiling rivers while I made laptop entries. What a team. Inland from the sea, the terrain was equally ragged and formidable, full of escarpments and bluffs. A mental vision arose of great ancient beasts sharpening monstrous claws, leaving proprietary raking marks.

Dry riverbeds traced the land contours and then flowed again with water as we approached Jabiru. On the East Alligator River, Jabiru—named for Australia's long-legged stork—is the site of the popular Alligator Hotel Resort, thematically crocodile shaped and very Disneyesque. The river was misnamed by Captain Cook—there are no alligators in Australia. Cook had it wrong. There are only crocs on this continent. Locals call it "Yellow Waters." Like Kipling's "great grey-green greasy Limpopo," it's alive with them. Our plan was to go wildlife spotting on the Jim Jim River the following day.

I was tightly wound about the Kakadu stopover, practically twitching in the cockpit over the chance to visit this famous sanctuary of stunning plants and exotic birds. As a young mother, intrigued by feathery flying things, I had kept a "life list" with Peterson Field Guide, logging my bird sightings. Once, touring New Zealand's Miranda Wildlife Preserve, we heard of the determined (obsessed?) German who arrived in a taxi from Wellington, asked to see the rare bent-beaked wrybill found only in New Zealand, checked off the sighting, and hopped back into his waiting cab for his flight back to Germany. I wasn't quite that addicted, but I had fanatically used a babysitter while I did some bird-watching. I understood his passion.

As we made a course change, our target red-earth Cooinda airstrip emerged in the distance. Down we idled, floating till tires chirped onto the runway, and taxied off onto the heat-miraged tarmac apron. The scorched pavement amplified and reradiated the midday temps, ramping down my excitement a notch or two. In the one patch of shade

sat the lone "Kakadu Air," a Cessna 207. Beside it, a waiting shed, optimistically latticed for any breeze. It was a necessarily brisk, very sweaty walk to the resort to escape the bush flies. We had to keep up the "Australian salute," the shooing wave-away of the little pests. It was fierce, how persistently they go for your perspiration—even worse, your moist eyes. At least they don't bite. Jerry donned his foreign legion hat.

The Kakadu Lodge grounds were steamy, lush, leafy, and tropical with wildlife ambling about. Right away, hot and hungry, we lucked into a welcoming open-air bistro.

But as we did, a large clip-tailed goanna sashayed menac-ingly by the tables, hips and tail switching back and forth. I bolted up onto a bench, entertaining our men enor-mously. They hee-hawed and swore that goannas don't bite—usually. Well, the goanna is a very large, formidable Australian monitor lizard with razor-sharp teeth and long claws—if not to attack and eat something, what were they for?

After a glass of tap beer and a mess of lovely hot, greasy, salty chips, we felt cheery and jolly. But after those chips and beer, Hal and I suffered a disgruntling downturn. Rooms were problematic—some had no functioning air conditioner. They had them, but they didn't work. A maintenance problem. Air conditioning was a necessary staple . . . a "must" in such a sweltering tourist location. At last, annoyed and exhausted, we checked into our *final* room—an hour and three moves in the blistering heat. The staff soothingly wooed us with a free bottle of wine at dinner. We mused as to how awesome a place the park must be, to be an attraction in such a furnace.

All would be revealed.

Ah, dinner. To the palate, the cuisine was close to *haute,* and even though sometimes puzzling, the menu delighted us with unusual dishes. The most notable: the dessert list's titillating *"Paris Breast."* All eyes were riveted on our waitress as she calmly pronounced the words with a straight face. So naturally we had to have it. It was an elegant puff pastry filled with sweet fruits and crème Chantilly. Good waitress—and she was a pilot. Gabriella had her commercial and instructor ratings, and her boyfriend flew that Cessna parked at the airstrip. Incredibly, she knew my friend and fellow pilot, the Australian CAA's Mary O'Brien in Bankstown. Like an old school tie, it was a happy connection. In her youth, Mary taught flying in China. Later, she was taken out by cancer. Rest in peace, Mary.

Out in the warm night, little lizards flattened themselves to the bistro ceiling, attracted to lights that served up a fluttering smorgasbord of moths. The moon was again that white luminous rocker in a deep black sky dense with brilliant near-equatorial stars. Beautiful, but oddly disquieting. Where were our familiar constellations? No North Star, no Ursa Major, no Cassiopeia, no Orion. We sure weren't in Kansas anymore. But there it was—the Southern Cross! When I was a child I'd lived in the post–World War II Philippines and been so puzzled, downright disappointed, not to see a dramatic twinkling cross in the sky, as though thickly encrusted with rhinestones. Now I could appreciate the astronomy better and the Cross's indication of where we spun in the universe.

THE AWESOME VIEW FROM OUR STARSHIP

Some places in the world are blessedly clear and clean of modern-day air pollution. The outback is such a place, providing glorious pristine night skies of inky blackness, nights of wonder, sharply spangled with stars, nights the ancient astronomers must have perused. Pondering and probing with their intellects, deeply curious about the positions and movements of the tiny lights in the heavens—the same stars and planets on which primitives built their imaginative theories of gods and foretelling.

URISINO

Another year, one of our stops found us at far-off Urisino Station, erstwhile estate of Sir Samuel Wilson, the nineteenth century's owner of the most sheep in Australia. Decades and interests passed. No longer a sheep station, at last an enterprising couple took over the once elegant homestead, abandoned and derelict. They created a special place where, besides road-traveling vacationers, touring pilots could come to enjoy an older era of outback history.

Aircraft navigate to Urisino's prominent red earth airstrip; there staff meets them with a handsome team of jostling camels pulling a wagon. Their large loose lips flap whimsically as they trot, thickly lashed eyelids drooping against the dust. Camels for work arrived long ago—starting out as early as Burke and Wills. When machines emerged to do their jobs, they were released into the wild. Later, some were rounded up for interesting uses, as at Urisino. There we put to rest the myth of the nasty, biting, spitting camel. We learned that camels are actually sweet-tempered and gentle, only made ornery by cruel treatment.

At day's end, we lay on our backs in the grass and marveled at the starry show, rueful that civilization had destroyed such beauty in our own country's night skies— except for maybe high in the Rockies. Once, while Bahamas-hopping, we flopped down late at night on a paved airstrip to spot satellites. (No night flying in the Bahamas.) Lovely, but nothing like Australia. Bahamian stars are dimmed by misty sea air.

The next morning at 6:45 AM there would be a river wildlife cruise in a low-slung motor boat. In view of the promised crocs, I thought I would not trail my fingers in the water.

By that night, there was a serious worry. Nick's condition—he was getting quite sick. Reggie rustled about among his pharmacopeias, dug out a bottle, and plied him with a miracle antibiotic.

He was a tough energetic Aussie, our leader Nick, and until this moment, no foolish medicine for him. But this bug had whacked him. Listlessly compliant, he finally welcomed the antibiotic.

We kept anxious fingers crossed for his recovery.

10 Green Ants and Bush Tucker

Oh no, please no, it just could not be. What a miserable start to our first Cooinda-Kakadu day. We were stupidly late to our dawn boat tour. Not for us, those thrilling trills and flutterings of a world awakening in densest glorious nature. A witless, inattentive communications glitch—we misunderstood the start time. It was our own fault. Clenching our hands, we glumly watched the boat pull away, leaving us behind. But, the accommodating staff, seeing our dismay, quickly and amiably shifted us to the sunset tour. "Why, that's truly better!" they promised. We so wanted to believe it.

Now we had to make do with extra space in our day. Quickly scoping out the morning's offerings, we scuttled and puffed a long kilometer down the road to join a nature walk with Ranger Sally. Sally quickly had her group peering deep into fronds of *Pandanus spiralis*, fronds that hid miniature tree frogs, and in the cause of "bush tucker discovery," had us testing nibbles of palm leaf bits. Enthusiastically, she urged the gutsiest of us to sample wriggling, citrusy green ants. "You have to pinch them up amidships to avoid fiery stings," Sally instructed. I grinned, responding, "I'll get you later if I do this and get dog-bit by some vile Aussie ant." But no worries . . . No sting. And being high in vitamin C, it actually did smack of lemon. She pointed out feral pigs' big mud wallows and the wide, bowl-like hollows of the water buffalo. She told us how the area totally changes with floods up to ten feet deep during the Wet (it's now the Dry). Bird-watching? It was overwhelming. I needed ball bearings for head swiveling. Besides sightings of five kinds of herons and several sea eagles to add to my life list, there were many, many others.

Lagoon-side, at a shady stop designed for tour spiels, from my position at the rear of the group, a sudden movement caught my eye. Disturbingly near us, an enormous croc noiselessly slithered into the water. Heart in my throat, I bellowed out warning. Panic rush! Terrifying thoughts came of drowning and rotting. Everybody scrambled, but humans apparently were not on his menu that morning. Don't count on it, though.

At the nature tour trail's end, a nice couple from Melbourne took pity on Hal and me—the temperature had soared to unbearable. The good-hearted Aussies drove us in their squishy air-conditioned car up to the Aboriginal Culture Center, a slick, informative place. And well air-conditioned.

That nice ride had dropped us and motored on, so after a bit we started trudging along the path back to the lodge—a hot, barely shaded wilderness trail. This was a typical season of the Dry, and trees were in self-preservation mode, quite sparsely leaved, the plant's way of staying alive and saving its water. Reggie and Brad happily came upon us there after their morning boat tour, and whispered our attention over to a couple of blasé black-crested cockatoos rendering tree seeds into meals.

Landscaper Brad, our *de facto* flora guide, gave us data about the local eucalyptus. In probing for information from the nearest bush, he touched a leaf to check its genus. Oops . . . Within a nanosecond he whizzed into short orbit, recoiling from a thousand attacking tasty green ants— critters that had been absolutely invisible until he jiggled the leaf. What reflexes! Both the ants' and Brad's. It was hilarious. Smiling to myself, I thought I wouldn't show him how to pick one up to eat it, as he was kind of busy hopping and whacking. It was astonishing how fast they mustered to defend that tree. A textbook symbiotic relationship: the tree feeds the ants and the ants protect the tree. It's a sharp-edged countryside. Who's the tucker here, anyway?

Late in the afternoon, the sunset cruise took us along the Jim Jim, the river that sprawls through the park's swampy flood plains. What we saw . . . we were spellbound. Huge crocodiles lay motionless on the banks, seemingly oblivious to strolling waterfowl that meandered randomly across their snouts, birds blissfully unmindful of any potential risk—unless it was moving. (Considering the balance of nature, could they be genetically programmed that way, so that sometimes the crocs can have a snack?)

An astonishing menagerie revealed itself, creature upon creature. There were herons, comb-crested jacanas and orange-crowned warblers all delicately treading the lotus pads. And plumed whistling brown ducks, little red-kneed dotterals, and "bumaroos"—the magpie geese that Aborigines like to pluck, split, and spread on fire to crisp up the fat. Makes a delectable feed. Bumaroo barbeque. To top it off, swooping across the river, flapping long graceful black wings and trailing long red legs, the elegant jabiru flew swift and low over it all. The jabiru is the only stork species found in Australia . . . We were astonished to see one right there on a close flyby. All the critters were in various stages of nesting—it was beautiful, enrapturing, springtime.

WATER LILIES and LOTUSES

Our open, uncanopied boat maneuvered carefully, gently, past numerous varieties of lush water lilies—from large, lilac-blossomed, tall-stemmed ones, to those bearing the tiniest snowflake flowers, and then we floated past a great showy stand of stunning Asian lotus in full rosy bloom, pushing up among spreading coolie hat umbrella leaves. Above it all, there was a gratifyingly ugly six-foot goanna, sunning on a tall dead trunk under the eyes of a sea eagle. The sun slipped low while birds settled in its coral glow, and dockward we puttered.

In talking with our guide, I found he'd been a ski instructor at Breckenridge, Colorado. Hmm. Snow. It will be discombobulating when we leave this hot springtime to take up life again in the icy chill of bare-tree autumn. In a few weeks, a Boeing 747 will speed us high over the earth's midsection, passing the Intertropical Convergence Zone, and in mere hours—presto change-o, where's your woolly coat?

Such extremes. Because the earth is what it is, what's steamy in one place is frozen in another.

Suddenly I had the memory of an Alaskan February flight—the ultimate wintertime, up around colossal Denali. That massif drew me like a magnet. As the years passed, the boys had grown, as they will, and my oldest had opted for a stint in the army. I had gone to visit our Anchorage-based son; I rented a plane for us to go prowling, crossing my heart somberly in the field operations office not to even think of going near the mountains. "There could be fierce downdrafts," they said, eyeing me worriedly. From the cockpit we surveyed a vastness of brilliant white snow and ice, void of all life but for the eye-catching motion of the occasional sled and huskies, mushing and training for the fabled Iditarod. The magnificent Alyeska Mountains towered at the edge of our view. Denali, aka Mount McKinley, rose in their midst, the whole range a giant wall at the end of the world. Stunning—powerful. Ah, but the day was perfectly calm, not a telltale ripple of wind or turbulence anywhere, and magnificently snow bright. Oh heck, I was irresistibly drawn to Denali. I'll stay twenty miles away, I said to myself, just in case. I'm adventurous but not stupid. The flight was of course way beyond the performance capabilities of the Cessna—we ran out of climb power at 14,500 feet, and Denali soared to over 20,200 feet. But we got a fine look and could feel its immensity even from our altitude.

INTERTROPICAL CONVERGENCE ZONE

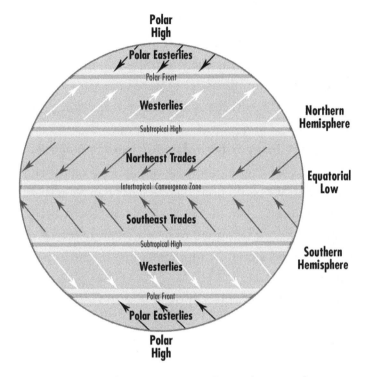

However, at that moment I fancied more the steamy sea-level greenery of Kakadu.

Dinner that night was convivial Aussie cook-it-yourself open BBQ–flavorsome scotch fillets (rib eyes) for Hal and me. The deal is this: you choose your meats and extras from a display case, pay the fare, and then take the meat to the grill and cook it yourself elbow-to-elbow with others with maybe a beer in hand. Homey and sociable. Over our plates we swapped tales and then headed back to our cabins along winding paths.

Thanks to Reggie's potent pills, Nick finally had arisen from his sickbed and, as the good host, led us down the paths by torch (flashlight), pointing its beam upward on some noisy fruit bats, their beady red eyes catching the light as they peered down on us. They're also called "flying foxes" for their little fox-like faces. Out in full force, they were busy dropping mango bombs off overhanging trees as they fussed and fed, plopping them onto paths and banging the tin-roofed bedroom units. They were intriguing to watch. As they grazed the overhanging mango trees, they plucked a fruit, took a bite or two, and dropped it from where they and the mangos both dangled from branches. They then scrambled over to the next mango and repeated, the entire night. We could not imagine what had been making the unsettling racket overhead, like left-footed burglars mucking about. It was good to have a mystery solved. This night we would sleep, thumpings dulled by the humming air conditioning.

The next day we would fly on, our senses saturated with resplendent, fecund nature.

11 ON TO MATARANKA

WE HAD TRACKED WELL across the
northern part of the continent, but still had far to go to
reach the other side. We were at what day . . . ten? Yes, the
tenth day, a third of the way around.

The continuing westbound flight to the next stop, the
Mataranka resort, was calculated to be long, and so about
halfway from Cooinda we would need to refuel at Tindal, a
military/civil installation. Since we were to do a bit of sightseeing en route, our path to refueling was not a direct line.
In calm winds, we took off eastward to track 139 degrees
southeast toward the cliffs of Jim Jim Falls, our first checkpoint. The curious name "Jim Jim" derives from the word
Anjimjim or the *Pandanus* palm trees lining the Jim Jim
River, that ubiquitous palm from which we plucked the
unlucky tasty tucker ant on our ecotour.

The dry, rugged landscape was sketchily visible through
a low-lying smoky layer, like ground fog—a stratified agricultural burn, perhaps. Anyway, being the Dry, the glorious
rushing falls had disappointingly disappeared for the
season. We took a course line for the fuel stop at Tindal.

Our flight took us over the impressive eons-carved Katherine Gorge and its winding river, making our way to Tindal's army base. Tindal has an MBZ for its military activity. That's a Mandatory Broadcast Zone, an extensive air traffic control area similar in size to those around Boston, Los Angeles, or New York City. This weekend it was NOTAM'd as "tower closed"—much easier for us. That merely meant no one was in the tower to advise us about landing sequences . . . we would simply announce ourselves and fly the way we always do at untowered fields (most airfields do not have control towers). The MOA (Military Operating Area) was also "cold." These kinds of special airspaces while in use are called "hot." Good thing it was cold—we were all tooling along awestruck and clueless, sightseeing right through it. Nick knew, but let us be happy, telling us later on where we'd been, with a little chiding to watch our charts.

As explained, west of the Great Dividing Range, all the way across to the far western coastal plain, there are no bucolic fields, no peaceful greenswards, no gentle green hills. And in this region there were also none of those wide flat clay pans for landing out—that euphemism for off-airport emergency landings.

Rough terrain continued unrelieved. Although always looked around for emergency landing spots, they were unforthcoming, and we tried not to think about it. Despite that, wherever we flew, it was a land whose overview was of delightful surprises and ever-changing textures. Each day we started out believing the country couldn't possibly offer anything else new. Each day we were proven wrong.

Ours was the fastest of the three convoy planes. It had

a postproduction replacement hopped-up engine . . . a plus in a couple of ways. We usually got there first, a nice position, whether we started before or after the rest. And second, because we arrived first we got to scope out the layout—figure out the "duty" runway (their word for "active")—the one everyone was using at that time, mandated the one facing the wind to provide a favorably slower ground speed for touchdown. We then began searching out parking tie-downs—a challenging job at confusingly large airports. Anyway, this all gave us the heady illusion of being all on our own. But at Tindal they were over-the-top helpful. A good thing, since it was puzzlingly laid out with military-style wide ambiguous taxiways and giant hangars. Although the MBZ was inactive, there was someone on the frequency to give directions.

ROYAL FLYING DOCTOR SERVICE

All down safely, we lined up at the bowser. But we had to wait—the Royal Flying Doctor Service was passing through on a mission, and they were put to the front of the line. They're the medical group the great outback heavily relies on, highly valued and esteemed, so no complaints. They deserved priority.

The RFDS was an idea conceived during World War I by young military pilots who saw aviation's potential in developing the outback. They especially envisioned airplanes as an aid to medicine—many people in the outlying regions of Australia, miners and early settlers, had not survived an injury or disease simply from lack of timely medical help. Bush hospitals, established by Presbyterian missionary minister John Flynn around 1912, began addressing the loneliness and desperation brought on by the extreme isolation, an isolation where illnesses and accidents were often grim death sentences. Bush hospitals were needed and welcomed, but transporting patients to them was often an insuperable problem, with time being an enemy and doctors few. With the advent of aviation in World War I, the remedy became clear—and finally in 1928 the Royal Flying Doctor Service began. It brought not just its 24-hour-a-day 365-day-a-year emergency service, but health care in general to all the outback. If a Flying Doctor's aircraft needed a top-off, we were glad to wait.

So on to Mataranka—resort of the crystal-clear everflowing thermal bath. But on climbout I had no airspeed readout, something required and useful for managing flight. I had flown without an indicator before, just by engine settings, but this was not my plane and we had a long way to go. A quick turn back to land. How tiresome. Sure enough, during our brief downtime a bug had found himself a refuge in the pitot tube (mounted on the wing, it faces forward and senses air ramming into it, part of the mechanism that tells you how fast the airplane is going).

Tiny insects are pesky enough, scouting for homes in aircraft pitot tubes, seriously clogging up the airspeed indicator system (sausage-like slip-on protectors are de rigueur at tie-down—as are air-

intake plugs that keep birds from nesting in the engine compartment).

But how about the bigger, in-your-face stinging kind? A hovering wasp can send the toughest guy whizzing in fear from not just pain, but the possibil-

ity of death ... from anaphylactic shock. So imagine me, yumpa-doo-dah, happily pottering along in the sweet little Cessna 150 flight school rental, nowhere to hide, nowhere to flee—and this huge fly crawls out of the panel and hums around in my space. But it's no fly, it's a tail-mounted stinger wasp. It heads back to the window and crawls up the windscreen in front of my disbelieving eyes ... and that wasp is followed by another, and another, and another ... Holy twitching sphincters! Panic! Panic! No, no, mustn't panic. Fly the airplane. No matter what, fly the airplane.

They mounted in ever-increasing numbers into my forward view, little feet clinging to the window, tiny antennae probing for escape. Where did they come from! It seemed like they were climbing out of the window defrost vent. Stings? "Rise above this ... Stay cool, stay calm," I said to myself ... "You don't want to crash and burn and embarrass yourself." My peripherals were alert, eyes taking in the horizon. Please, no jerking reflexes to pitch the plane into out-of-control maneuvers. With the corners of my eyes I glanced around for something, anything, to start methodically smashing them. Intently, calmly. Cold sweat. Mustn't rile them. Tricky stuff, keeping them from buzzing about the cockpit and homing in on me. Always careful not to lose track of where I was in the air. My dad had said, "Never take your eyes off your aircraft's attitude for more than a couple of seconds. Things can get away from you." Okay then, here's a wadded up paper towel. (I always fly with paper towels for preflight oil dipstick wipes when checking oil quantity.) "Now, don't hesitate," I muttered to myself. "Go on, reach forward with that wad and smash the first one." Yessss! The rest didn't notice as they were so focused on finding egress. Now the second, now the third, and so on, and so on, with teeth clenched and shoulders bunched till they were all killed—at least those I saw—all the time keeping my bird pretty straight and level. A straggler or two lumbered up the windscreen, but by now I realized they just wanted out—like me.

I arrived back at my base, landed carefully, shot like a rocket from the cockpit in case any leftovers would follow me in fury, and raced to the mechanic to spew out my angst, telling him all about it. Turned out, at some point a cloud of wasps swarmed to nest in the tail section of the quietly parked aircraft. They naturally got stirred up by the engine's vibration, left their home in the once-tranquil dimness, wended their way forward through the fuselage to the engine compartment, and hiked up to the light—right there in front of me. Well, the Cessna 150 is a small airplane. They didn't have far to poke about. The mechanics had to take apart the whole fuselage to get rid of them.

Moral: Be prepared. You never know what might be coming next. And never panic.

A fast ream-out fixed our Tindal event, and off we taxied for takeoff. Tower communications accomplished, we rolled.

Nick, however, chose this moment to get feisty and macho with the woman pilot. We were communicating well with the tower about crossing vehicles way farther down the runway, which he had not heard. He lambasted me for taking off . . . We had succinct words. Don't mess with Texas, you know? He was rarely a jerk, but this was an affront. Guess he wasn't all better—maybe.

We cruised at two thousand feet. It was a fairly unmonitored and lonely territory, so somewhere along the way, we chopped power and dropped down to examine traces of once-active railroad tracks. They were sure enough defunct, but a major road running alongside sported an occasional "road train"—truck cabs pulling two, three, or four trailers hooked together—now the country's alternative main freight system.

So spectacular when they buckle and flip.

And more termite mounds.

Trees began to flesh out the landscape as we drew nearer to the rustic Mataranka resort; what a pleasure to have this overview, revealing the changes slowly happening below us. We finally made out the oasis, thickly festooned with towering palms marking the pool and Roper River waterway. Arriving at the backdoor dirt strip, I did a low, slow pass to check out runway conditions. Seemed fine. So I executed a 180-degree turn into short final and flared to touch down.

What's this? No time to think! Reacting quickly, banking wings this way and that, I tiptoed to wheel-dodge the odd little termite mound, surprise, surprise. They could do some serious damage, so I called a heads-up to the others. No dramas. Unnerving for us, but apparently not unusual for Aussie dirt strips.

In the outback, these gigantic post-like anthills are as common as bush flies. Forget the iconic kangaroo—the termite could be the nation's symbol. Their high-rise colonies grow absolutely wherever, peppering hectares upon hectares of sweeping desert desolation. The termite/ant is not finicky—and he's extraordinarily ubiquitous. An open airstrip or a roadside shoulder can serve nicely as well as vast expanses in the deserts. We had been totally fooled at our first aerial sight of the mounds. We thought there must have been a widespread flood that had left mud on a forest burn-off, coating the stumps. Nope. Not stumps. Nick explained it all later on.

The Mataranka resort was picturesque, in an open-air out-west way. RVs rolled in for rooms or campsites, either one. Since we landed around back behind the lodge, we entered by the only visible door—at the kitchen. We arrived out where they tossed the junk. Clearly not much fly-in business. It was awkward.

No glad-handing welcoming committee. Nobody but a tight-lipped cook who seemed off-put about our invading his domain. We timidly made our way through his kitchen, around his cooking pots and out, and then poked through an empty service area until, relieved, we came upon the office. There, somebody showed up to point us to our rooms. We later found the postcard presentation view and the "Welcome, Mates!" front desk, around where you *drive* in, all spilling over with spectacular bougainvillea.

Bags sweatily dragged to our digs, we beelined to the shady café, cathedral ceilinged with huge beams. Open air. Hot. But with fans. And ahhh, the mandatory icy beer . . . and juicy buffalo burgers. It was all good. Then off to the famous pristine thermal pools.

The waterway lay down a winding tropical path, a pool that soon glimmered through the trunks of magnificent towering date palms. Their lovely rippling reflections played below on shade-dappled waters. Easing our bodies into the natural pool was beyond therapeutic—the delicious sensation of those clear warm waters approached bliss. The hot spring pool was crystal clear, the waters naturally flowing in at one end of the pool and out the other for constant cleansing and replenishing.

Interesting sidenote—it turned out this oasis attracted multitudes of noisy fruit bats. Here they sought out ripening dates, fat bunches hanging heavy, sweet, and convenient. Bats spent the days clustered and screeching, thoroughly infesting the palms and rising in occasional bursts of leathery-winged flight. So much for bats sleeping in the daytime. Cute little foxy faces, but a bat is a bat. We mused about their voiding upside down and found it repulsive. However, bat-repelling devices kept the swimming areas clear of them; they were not an issue.

Enjoying the waters, Nick pointed out a familiar-looking muscular blond, a big-jawed athletic type. Turned out he was the Eveready Battery dude, an erstwhile ace Aussie football player and total alpha male. Swimming toward him, I asked, "Don't you do those battery ads in the United States? Never thought I'd see you here!"

A typical celebrity jock, he liked being noticed. "It's a small country." He grinned amiably. "There aren't that many people!" He then turned his attention to a goo-goo-eyed nubile beauty, hovering in his wake. Nick said he has a nationwide reputation for working his way through willing females. Each day had its surprise.

After a fine splash, a shady path beckoned. Nick motioned for us to come for a hot ramble through some deep woods, taking us to a hidden river site called "Stevie's Hole." He knew a lot, but I wasn't sure about this. Each inch of the way we dealt with swarming clouds of relentless tiny bush flies craving moisture from our sweat and most annoyingly from our eyes. At least they didn't want to suck blood. They were worse than flies around a horse, and us without a tail to flick. Draping towels around our heads and waving the Australian salute, we scurried our way to relief.

Escape came in the hidden swimming hole, quiet and deeply shaded by huge airy paper gums (melaleucas). To our happy astonishment, a sulfur-crested cockatoo moved cautiously down through the shadows to drink, sipping from a water-skimming branch. Wallowing in the cool water till we were chilled and shriveled, we finally braced ourselves to rejoin the one-hundred-degree heat and mosey back to the bistro for VBs and our pals.

Later, dinner was a full-feast buffet on the terrace, romantically sheltered by spreading fan palms, under the dome of our wraparound galaxy.

12 KUNUNURRA

WONDERFUL WORD. THE LAST *u* is a de facto "ah." We pondered the indigenous Aussie names. Why would Aboriginal words be used by settlers trying to make their new home their own? Lots of British names of course, such as Sydney, Cairns, New South Wales, etc. Initially the immigrants had little to do with the natives, except to wildly slaughter and malign them. Did you know at one point there was a bounty on the Aborigine? How ghastly, how foul. How brutal, how sad. Of course some tribes themselves were hideously cruel. Males pitilessly tortured women. And why? Because they could. As the nineteenth-century missionary hymn went, "Where every prospect pleases, and only man is vile."

We Yanks also have place names with homegrown origins—some states for example. Half of them have relics of American Indian culture (start with Massachusetts and Connecticut). Never mind the plethora of towns and rivers. But our own are so familiar we don't notice.

We left behind Mataranka's warm pools and busy fruit bats for Kununurra, a large town on the northeastern edge of the Kimberley. To avoid rough air, we were off and flying early. The SOP for comfortable hot weather touring: takeoff before the thermals start their upward spiraling. They are fun updrafts for circling in to gain altitude, but uncomfortable to bump through from one side to the other, one after the other.

The Kimberley is the immense wilderness region of complex geography occupying much of northwestern Australia. Kununurra had a good modern airport, a welcome sight after traveling above extended stretches of rugged earth, stone, and trees—with not a single spot for an emergency landing. Oh, we had complete faith in our planes, but . . .

Kununurra. Here were Australian diamonds! Outlets were here for the huge Argyle diamond mine, itself available for tours. But our guys were not interested in pricey baubles. I was quite outnumbered. I didn't mind. Reggie and Brad herded us to Tourist Information to look for a different expedition. Hmm . . . A Dawson boat tour on the Ord River, famous for splendid persimmon-red vistas with dappled aqua waters and odd little flats of floating islands. That set, we ducked out of the sun into a shady pub for a cool beer and then found a bakery with luscious sandwiches and meat pies, good for a walking lunch back to the hotel. Phooey with diamonds. Sour grapes can be good.

Whitney Dawson's van came around to collect us for transfer to the dock, joining others on his canopied boat. Soon we were kicking up a good wake down the Ord, gaping at dramatic beauty carved through eons from orange-rose granite.

Whitney was angry with the authorities. He was a big affable guide who liked to please. The town fathers had clipped his wings by prohibiting free beer for his customers—said he was selling liquor without a license (via the tour fee), avoiding paperwork and taxes. Can't get around greedy governmentals wherever they can flex muscles. A license for everything. Never mind—he loaded us up with "tea time"—his wife's mouthwatering raisin bran muffins, local fruits, and an "eski" (Eskimo ice chest) filled with sodas. Big buff Whitney was a complex repository of local history and eco-data. He kept a well-crafted spiel running while navigating smooth waters between soaring views of massive red ravines.

FLOATING ISLANDS

The river bluffs held whimsical fat *boabs* (smooth, bulging bottle trees, their thin crooked bare branches waving yellow flower tufts); *kapoks*, vertical sheets of sinuous roots pushing out from the trunks, rising half submerged from the earth; a full contingent of herons on the floating islands (drifting mats of vegetation dense enough to support small animal life); and grinning crocs lolling indolently on the banks.

The Ord, a waterway dammed up to provide a reliable water source for local agriculture, had an ever-constant water level, making a stable riverbank ecology possible. Thick stands of rushes edging its banks would often break loose. The larger mats provide roomy nesting and feeding places for waterfowl.

Something was provocatively unclear. If they're floating islands, they must drift with the river flow. Where do those bird towns end up? We never found out.

One island inched along almost imperceptibly, moving up and down gently on swells, transporting wonderful creatures like the endearing little yellow lap-cheeks. These shared the pad with whistling ducks and black-fronted dotterels. Cute little lap-cheeks . . . long spindly legs and wee yellow cheek pouches, alongside the tiniest of birds, the dainty little dotterel that can practically walk on the very water itself, with its funny wide spidery feet.

The Ord, its banks nearly as profuse with wildlife as Kakadu Park's Jim Jim River, sported the occasional fisherman and Jet Skier. That activity was minimal—the area was natural and undeveloped. We felt like we were in a time warp.

An interesting trick of the settlers' ingenuity: by merely crowding banana trees to create the needed humid environment, they were able to raise bananas successfully—never before heard of in this sort of climate and always deemed impossible.

At tour's end we chugged to the Ord River Dam to admire the sunset while it did a slow fiery flameout and slipped into darkness. Whitney dropped us at our motel, where Nick was waiting with an icy six-pack. Good man. (If it seems like we're quaffing a lot of beer, don't worry—we were sweating it out as fast as we drank it.) We tossed those down and then trooped down the road to prime chopstick Chinese at the Country Club Resort. With two bankers at the table, Hal and Reggie, we attacked and chewed over current economics. It was interesting to get another world perspective. Finally, we let go of our chopsticks, and Reggie and Brad went out on the town before turning in.

For all that the night was to bring us, we should have gone with them. But Hal and I hit the sack.

We began to doze . . . and then jerked up in an electrified panic! Our room's fire alarm went off! What—? Hmm. No smoke and no fire. Well, that's good, anyway.

Except nothing, but *nothing*, would stifle the shrieking alarm. The high-tech smoke detector in the ceiling had suddenly gone haywire, screeching a brain-piercing, unremitting warning, pulsing rhythmically, filling all airspaces. Feckless hotel staff showed up to wring their hands helplessly (two sweet but useless women). We took turns standing and teetering, bouncing on the bed to reach it, a *de facto* trampoline, wobbling and waving our arms like windmills in frantic, futile efforts to smack it, kill it. And then—we *tricked* it. We shut it up by turning the ceiling fan on full bore to blow on it and cowered under the covers. I don't remember whose idea that was, or why it worked exactly, but it was brilliant. Ripping it out had been my plan.

And so we slept.

13 BUNGLE BUNGLE -> MOUNT HART

ANOTHER TAKEOFF, NOW FOLLOWING the river to the huge, shimmering aquamarine Lake Argyle, framed by spectacular red-coral mountains, and then directly to the Bungle Bungle wilderness reserve.

At Nick's tactful on-frequency heads-up, "You might want to avoid the Em Bee Zed, there's traffic inbound," we whip-jerked away from fixating on the scenery, veering left. It was so seriously desolate, it was easy to forget how common, if not constant, air traffic was in this area. Ahead, there was a prescribed flight path for cruising the curiously named Bungle Bungle, the next waypoint on our GPS.

The Bungles may be the strangest geology we've yet encountered: an extensive area of carved, shmoo-like beehive formations of black- gray and rust-layered strata, eroded into a jigsaw of smoothly rippled cliffs, bulging geo-bodies, and twisting canyons. They took 350 million years to form. Bizarre—and beautiful. Photographs don't tell it. And although a road passed for years within no distance at all of them, they were so hidden that they were not known to anyone other than the Aborigines until the 1980s. A pilot then marked a way in by dropping flour bags from a plane along the most likely access. There's a rudimentary four-wheel-drive dirt road in there now.

For all the history of Australia, until the twentieth century when overflying military noticed them and got an explanation from the Aborigines, they were not known to the white man. (However, the Army, being the Army, never told the world about them.) Late in his retirement, after our return from our Australian flyabout, we reported in to my USAF command pilot father. He sat with us to hear about the trip . . . his eagle eyes riveted on me. He examined my face intently. He then asked, "Did you see the Bungle Bungles?" My scalp prickled. In all the years, he had never spoken of them. And I had not heard of them before I got there. You see, in World War II when he fought in the South Pacific, he and his squadron had been privy to something remarkable while maneuvering over Australia, and he clearly hoped that I too had seen what he once saw.

Funny how they remained such a secret. Well, they are intriguingly inaccessible and best seen by air.

Departing the Bungle Bungle, we groped our way west through low visibility in the smoke from wildfires, but the air cleared as we headed upwind beyond the smoldering in the King Leopold Mountains. Continuing on toward Mount Hart—over mountains whose orographic influence put even more vertical components into the already turbulent day, holding altitude wasn't a problem—but keeping our heads from whacking the headliner was. We climbed a few thousand feet hoping for smoother air and less chop, but it was a waste of time.

MOUNT HART

Mount Hart, a surprising lush oasis in the middle of arid mountains, is fed by mountain streams from Mount Matthew Gorge. For this stop, we needed the GPS—one mountain crest looked exactly like the next—and after more than three hours of being batted around by frisky midday winds and thermals, we were thankful to spot that hard-packed gravel strip, invitingly tucked between ridges. Down we came over the trees, happy to put wheels onto land again.

Taffy, our genial host, greeted us enthusiastically as we rolled to a stop, quickly corralling us for the grand tour. Mount Hart, its low bungalows a remote retreat from the world, was created from scratch, turf to trees, by a succession of owners over the years. There was no local electricity; Mount Hart's came from its own generator, turned off at night. The verdant little valley resort catered to fly-ins, but access by car was easy from the west-coast town of Broome (we stopped at Broome later). Sara from England was our chef, and lunch was gustatory bliss. How to get this intake under control? Skip brekkie, skip lunch. Skip living. We dozed in the afternoon to make up for the upsetting night before, then feasted again as Sara flaunted her dinner stuff. Couldn't win.

The tropical sunset came suddenly, with night rapidly following as if somebody had rolled down a shade. With that came the dinner call. Hal, Reggie, and Brad had gotten in a walk, a paddle, and a swim, so that set them up quite well for the high-calorie gourmet spread. I had just lolled and absorbed the atmosphere. Anyway, the shallow swimming hole in the creek hadn't looked so good to me. A floating bit of trash had turned me off. Upsetting how that stuff shows up in the nicest places.

Now to rest and think about our day before nodding off. Oh, but first a little drama. Ha! There were vigorous wee frogs hopping erratically about our room. Whee!

Hal had ambled out to stargaze on the airstrip, but the moonlight was so intense it washed out the sky and lit up the earth, throwing menacing black shadows into the footpath. Thinking better of it, he sloped back to our room, just in time for a frog to leap up and peg itself to his bare calf. It then arced onto the bed as he shook it off. We could *not* catch it—and, *hello*—there were more! How cute, how maddening.

We hollered for Nick, who rallied to shoo out the lot—actually only three or four—but they were fast-moving targets. One comically launched up to his balding head and stuck there. Nick was Mr. Cool. He chuckled, grabbed it, and showed us how, when he was a kid, he would pop one into his mouth and walk up to grown-ups with the froggy-face bulging out between his lips. I think Mother had her hands full with little Nickie.

Located on the Barker River in the middle of the King Leopold Range, Mount Hart Wilderness Lodge Resort had developed in stages. A few of its seriatim entrepreneurial owners had "Cattle Baron" on the brain . . . but they hadn't thought it through. After a grand fattening-up on lush acreage, the on-hoof drive to market reduced the bulked-up cattle to near skeletons—not too saleable. No railroad for the transit. And then there were the droughts.

The owner in 1954 brought in many nifty varieties of trees and planted green turf, creating a serene garden oasis. Lizards and birds clearly loved it—it was a haven from the heat, being twenty degrees cooler in the shade. Birds populated the resort in impressive numbers and varieties, their colorful darting flights and distinctive birdcalls endlessly appealing.

The lodge was fitted out with painted cement floors (cool underfoot) and a tropical-style elevated roof and eaves—everything screened for easy airflow. Supplied with large fans, the living area had comfortable rattan for lounging, luxuriant green leaves brushed the windows, lizards streaked across the screens, and birds trilled those melodious songs. And then in the nighttime stillness, dingoes started up a mournful howling.

Taffy had coaxed a couple of dingoes in from the wild to be pets—which worked, sort of. The dingo is a happy-go-lucky, amiable wild dog, but maddeningly untrainable. And they're nimble. As a pup, one had climbed up onto a plane and chewed off an antenna. They can climb like cats. They're a bit like coyotes, but bigger.

In the common room stood a handsome wooden table for guests' use—I later settled there to update my log, in the area where Taffy set the coffee station and supplied a refrigerator with extra water. But the electricity signed off promptly at 10:00 PM and then no more lights. It was scurry-to-bed time. He kept a twelve-volt battery system going for minilamps and minifans rigged at the head of each bed—but it could run only one thing at a time. Read or be cool. We settled for the lulling, cooling, soft hum of the fan.

Nighttime in the Kimberley, and for the moment the dingoes were quiet. I hoped they weren't gnawing antennas.

That was my last drowsy thought before I realized dawn was coming. A very good sleep.

14 BROOME

AS DAY CREPT UP on Mount Hart, I got up to poke about and find coffee makings in the half-dark lounge. Taffy had already set it out for us—maybe his light step had awakened me. Reggie was up to the same, so we poured our cups and took them onto the porch for some quiet conversation. Such good company, our Aussie banker. What an excellent place—our favorite kind. The wildlife began its dawn stirrings while we sipped and talked. I would miss such moments.

And so it was again Hal's turn at the yoke. Charts reviewed at breakfast, we hauled bags to our airplanes, pushing our way out of the shade through sunny swarms of bush flies. Preflights done—no dawdling—we flew away from their insistent swarming. Climbing up and away over thick forests and mountains, we headed west, leaving windows open to blow out leftover flies and swatting at those who didn't get the hint. Adios, Chef Sara; bye-bye, Taffy; and same to the dingoes—who by the way had not, in the night, performed atrocities upon our planes. Mount Hart had been another unique stopover in an astonishing lineup.

We were going to Broome via the Buccaneer Archipel-ago, along the rugged Kimberley coast, a place where high tides made huge spilling waterfalls. By and by the hazy distant Indian Ocean segued into view, the rugged terrain below us stopping abruptly in plummeting cliffs at the sea, forming coves and little shell-shaped beaches, opening up to the beautiful islands and bays of the archipelago.

We had now crossed the entire continent.

At the coastline, we turned south to track for Broome. There was nobody out there. Nobody. How curious. Miles upon miles upon miles absolutely untouched by concrete or blacktop. No settlements—no coastal road—not even a footpath to the waterside. The reason: most of these coastal waters don't support much fish life. The runoff from the desert continent is not nutrient rich, so neither are the waters. Never mind . . . for us the visuals were enough.

Here the ocean was rimmed by astonishing red and purple rocky shores heavily carved with crescent beaches, streaked with curiously patterned sandbars.

Islands sat offshore, part of Buccaneer Bay; one had remnants of mines. Reggie pointed out a Paspaley Company pearling boat and their pearl farms—lacy grids of cabling attached to the surface by floats, like a carefully flung trap. After a delicate and complicated seeding of baby oysters—tiny ones scooped by divers off the ocean floor and strung on special panels from the cables, they are left for pearl cultivation. Large tides of unpolluted waters in this cyclone-free area feed the bivalves a rich mixture of organic food. *(So there's enough nutrition to feed oysters, anyway.)* After careful harvesting, the oysters are reseeded and replaced for the next crop. It's a thriving industry—Paspaley pearls are Australia's answer to Japan's Mikimoto.

A solitary yacht was at anchor in a tiny remote cove, very still, no signs of life. Why, and who? Reggie said it had to be a drug dealer, so far away from everything. Looking down into Beagle Bay we noted two large submarine-like shapes moving through the water—sharks, not whales . . . no flukes. Even from our safe altitude, those shadowy forms made us shiver. We continued down the west coast.

And now, throttling back a bit, the descent into Broome.

"All stations Broome, Em Bee Zed, Sierra Charlie Uniform, Cessna one seven two, twenty miles north of Broome at fifteen hundred feet, estimating joining the circuit at twenty-three past the hour."

A wide runway beckoned for landings. Whispery touch-down, taxi in, join the bowser queue for fuel. Roll the planes into parking spots, hop into a van, and head for the Tropi-cana Inn—and there we were . . . A moment for laundry and grabbing lunch at their pub. Everything normal, a pretty place, nothing out of the ordinary.

Well, not yet. Who could know?

It came later.

Hal toured the little museum across the street, giving a *précis*, "a charmingly naive presentation of the town's extraordinary history as a pearling center." Nick and the techno-geek went off to do their particular things; we jumped into a taxi with Brad and Reggie to scope out the fabled Cable Beach Resort and watch the sunset from its ocean-view veranda.

Settling ourselves under a deck umbrella, we ordered drinks and stared across putting-green grasses. I rubbed my eyes . . . What an incongruous sight: flitting ballet dancers pirouetting along the greensward in warm-ups, silhouetted against the sea. It turned out the Western Australia Ballet Company was booked for the next night, and the roadies were setting up. Our eyes widened more, as fourteen highly tasseled and brocaded dromedaries came lurching and sloping in behind them, noses high, strung out along the near horizon. How wonderfully bizarre. Camel rides were a touted resort specialty. We just never knew what we were going to see. (No, that was not the aforementioned *it*.)

The deck filled up, the sun lingered on the far horizon, and we hustled back to a motel dinner featuring succulent Moreton Bay bugs—small "slipper" lobsters, delicacies commonly found in northern Australia and some other parts of the Pacific. Bedtime at nine thirty . . . comfy sleeping to the humming air conditioner and then bounce up for breakfast on the upper deck, a full hot breakfast eye level with gecko-loaded palms and a flamboyant flowering African tulip tree. Next, a tour of the town via City Tours, in a funky bus, artistically painted with colorful local scenes.

THE BENDS, A NACRE CHURCH, GAUTHEAUME POINT

After peering at the old pearling boat jetty, we toured the Japanese cemetery where victims of the once mysterious and devastating "bends" ended up, hapless pearl divers who long ago came from Japan for work, diving and dying for the button industry. Yes, pearls were a big deal back then—but *mother-*

of-pearl was even bigger—a basis of the preplastic button industry. Huge business. Some may remember buttons that annoyingly broke in half at the thread holes. Those had been made from delicate oyster shell mother-of-pearl nacre, the coating of the inside of the shells, a secretion that also creates pearls. There were photos of a king-tide street flooding, the semiannual big tide . . . not a bad miss. We looked in at an extraordinary mother-of-pearl church altar, crafted from iridescent shell linings.

And then came the unique, dazzling shoreline at Gantheaume Point. That was, for me, the raison d'etre of the stopover. That is where deeply water-sculpted, truly purple-red rock strata and tidal pools met pearly beaches— and the startlingly blue Indian Ocean. Red, white, and blue had never been so spectacular.

Oh—that wasn't *it*, either.

THE LOCK-UP

The main landmarks surveyed, we spun off from the group to be on our own. Seeking local advice, we were steered to the charming, out of the mainstream Lock-Up Café—a creative reuse of Broome's historical gaol (jail —Brit hangover) site. The restaurant was the project of the chef and her husband, who had knocked together handsome tables from old ships' timbers. Again we hit the jackpot . . . its sunny patio, fat pots of fragrant flowers and herbs positioned here and there. We were offered up a sandwich lunch of luscious homemade bread, crispy sausage rolls, salad with juicy full-flavored homegrown tomatoes, and aromatic steeped iced tea. We had not gone to the hotel to eat with the rest, and Nick was annoyed. He sniffed and grumbled that we couldn't have found anything worth eating anywhere else. Silly man. Too bad. It was our adventure, no? His humor, as I have said before, was under a strain.

Never mind. That was just after *it*, which probably had the effect of further jangling his good nature.

So, here it is then, exactly how *it* was.

15 IT

When in time we returned to the hotel, something odd was afoot. We found our men out by the pool on chaise lounges, inside the enclosure. Our geek hushed us, his back to us and his chin hanging over the chain-link fence, peeking in. What's this? A photo shoot. Jerry advised us *sotto voce* the pool was closed, off-limits. Oh? Not to us—we were paying customers. In we went—but quietly. The rest of the guys were slumped behind newspapers, slack-jawed at poolside, watching. And what were they looking at, you ask?

I turned around. At the other end of the pool, the focus of a bank of lights and cameras on tripods, was a string-bikinied piece of eye candy with tossing black curls, big blue eyes, china-doll complexion, and an hourglass figure—the kind most fellows would like to have on their arms—or in them. She was sprawled across a fringed bench swing. I smiled and called out, "Wow, you're beautiful!"

She waved happily, lolled seductively back, and when her photographer said to do it—she plucked off the teeny bra and bottom. Totally naked, she then arched her back to thrust rosy nipples in the air and lowered her eyelids to come-hither levels, opening full lips in a lazy half smile. She let her knees fall apart, feet lifting erotically into the air. She then strained and stretched her thighs wide open and thrust her hips upward, maximizing the allure of her wide-open privates—magnificently displayed in the bright photo lights—showing off all she had in front of God and everybody. The tip of her tongue traced her lips.

And then—Holy Mother of God—she reached down to touch herself.

Our men's breathing seemed to stop, their eyes now burning holes in the newspapers they were pretending to hide behind. Tension hummed in the air. The shoot ended shortly, leaving them somewhat off-kilter, I'm sure.

It turned out it was the Australian version of Playboy in a playgirl photographic session. (Porno Down Under?) Now how did *that* happen on our beat? Nick had to be in a high-speed wobble.

And that was *it*.

To some, maybe not so much. But it was sincerely discombobulating—so out of context, so utterly unexpected.

THE *CORNELIUS*

It was also good that we were heading right out on a sunset cruise on a grand old pearling lugger.

A stabilizing diversion. The antique lugger was a gaff-rigged, handsome, rust-red-sailed ketch, this one used

during the twilight of the mother-of-pearl business.

The *Cornelius*, our vessel, was a fifty-year-old beauty configured now for pleasure outings up and down the shore along the extensive gleaming white Cable Beach.

Boarding her was a challenge. Our large vanful needed three tender-loads (a tender is a small boat) to transport us, including elders who had lost the agility to clamber easily from surf, to tender, to boat (and back again later in the full dark). Awkward even for the nimble, it took many steadyings and "heave-hos" before they made it . . . Not a junket for the frail or creaky.

Ah, but these frail elders reminded me of someone. When I was a new pilot logging hours of flying about for fun, I came across an old guy at the neighboring airport. Then in his seventies and quite palsied, Cliff had earned his license fifty years before. Back then, attracted by his der-ring-do, a young lady lured him into marriage. Afterward came a revelation . . . his wife did not want him to fly. He first thought it was the cost and began to build his own wings in the basement. Well no, she sobbed . . . she was simply terrified of his flying. So, angel man that he was, for his adored bride he gave up flying entirely.

When I met Cliff, she had just passed on. Her body was barely cool in the ground when he showed up at the airport.

He told me his story. Clearly, after all those years, he needed the overview; I invited him to go flying right there on the spot. Eagerly, if shakily, he dragged himself up and in on all fours—and off we went for a quick flight around the area. We did that a few times over the next months. Time passed. One day I came to the airport—and was greeted by a cheery old Cliff gleefully waving his fresh license. He had passed his FAA-required physical exam, taken refresher flying lessons, and now was a new man. Well, whether he knows it or not, a widower is surely in the market for a new wife . . . and a bosomy little widowed blue-hair snapped him up. And this gal loved to fly. They were happily married for four years, until one day Cliff flew on over that far horizon of no return. Happy ending for Cliff.

So bravo and kudos for the spirit in those seniors.

Generous hors d'oeuvres circulated and beer made its way into eager hands. Shortly, the *Cornelius* rolled gently under billowing sails as she made way, and we chatted with the shipboard group for an agreeable couple of hours. A New Orleans couple's son had met and romanced an Aussie gal online, and they had just been to their wedding.

The sun slipped toward the horizon in flaming flamingo pink, and we began the slow going-home process, load by load. Returning to shore involved nervous wading in moonlit surf in the shallows (what was in there?) from tender to beach. Gorgeous. Cable Beach may be the longest and most beautiful beach in the world—the flat white silky sand stretches for at least a half mile before it even meets the sea. Its utter flatness made for a long gentle surf all along its thirty-five-mile length—ideal for RVs, with acres and acres of space between. In the moonlight, we stopped at a family group to chat and take pictures of their excited kids and their just-caught shovelhead shark. Hmm. Had we known, we would have been terrified about wading. An odd-looking creature. But not big. At least not that one.

What a wild, kaleidoscope day. And the next, on to the mining community of Port Hedland, a stop en route to Perth—Perth of the famous King's Park Botanic Gardens, the infamously cruel Fremantle Jail, and the WA/SA Symphony (Western Australia/Southern Australia). In Perth we would spend three full days. We would not tour Port Hedland—a new town of industrial mining properties. It would just be a resting place along the long track southward from Broome. No problem with that.

16 PORT HEDLAND

THIS DAY HAL AND I were ready to roll first. So we hummed out of Broome over Roebuck Bay. (The *Roebuck* was the name of an especially vicious pirate ship.) Our track to Port Hedland took us over 260 miles of phenomenal, undeveloped beaches—undeveloped because there was no freshwater anywhere. We spotted rare dirt paths along the shore, which seemed to go to small boat launching areas—but there was not one soul in sight. Even a few old research sheds were abandoned. We, seeing it from above, could not get over the mesmerizing cobalts and aquamarines of the seas. Maybe great scenery wasn't enough to surmount the desolation—and the issue of the lack of fresh water. (In the Bahamas they solve that by tankering it in.)

Our tracks and altitudes varied playfully—we were carefree, wheeling and soaring, diving and climbing—like sea birds. It was truly deserted, uninhabited, with absolutely no other air traffic. We swooped down to three hundred feet over the smooth cusp of creamy sand and sparkling sea for a close-up and then soared up, up to four thousand feet for the overview. Brad called out a pod of whales plunging and breeching—a couple of big ones and a calf. Otherwise, the only visible life was a possible turtle and a few startled flocks of surf-feeding birds. They rose and darted away in unison, like skittish schools of minnows. We knew there was multiple animal life there, but we just couldn't see it no matter how we strained. The disadvantage of the aerial view.

Flying low, we scanned for wildlife and then—too bad— the GPS bellied up again. Well, no dramas—the PD (Port Hedland) nondirectional beacon was alive and, as our joking Aussies said, "just keep the ocean on the right." A musty old saw for coastal folks. Easily spotted landmark— gigantic salt-drying beds marking the fifteen-mile MBZ call-in point. We called the UNICOM for the duty runway, but no response. Continued on, checked the wind sock, picked runway thirty-two pointing northwest toward the coast for the headwind—the onshore breeze—announced our intentions, landed, and taxied in. Still nobody.

Where to park? The airport appeared to be deserted. Getting rattled, we meandered on featureless wide ramps past huge hangars, searching futilely for someone, anyone, for guidance. Holiday weekend, nobody home, nobody in the tower . . . looked like Scotty had beamed everybody up.

Ah . . . Across the concrete a man emerged from an outfit called Polar Aviation and hailed us. Our engine noise had flushed him out. We confessed sheepishly in drawling American how we had no idea what the Port Hedland SOPs could be . . . Could he help? Tower on holiday, no helpful "Transient Parking" signs, no line of tied-down planes as a hint. Where should we go? "Oh right over there," he pointed cheerfully, waving us over *there*—"facing the RFDS hangars. That'll be good." And so we did. He said he had worked outside of Chicago.

Seemed fine and straightforward, right?

But when he arrived finally, Nick could hardly contain his fury. He didn't exactly hop, but he bobbed about and waved his upper limbs. He did not like where we had parked, and he let us know about it. What was that about? I resisted flipping him a pithy hand gesture. Why hadn't he explained beforehand what he wanted? I don't think he actually knew. He was just itching to blow up. He was way, way stressed out, maintaining the host and guide role despite his other preoccupations. It was clear that Hal and I, and *things*, were getting on his nerves. Only two weeks out, and two to go. Oh boy.

And it seemed that Jerry, Nick's compu-geek plane mate, as stated at the outset, was ungenerous. While flying along he would furtively dip into his box of crackers and not offer any to Nick, while Nick would always kindly share his own snacks. Jerry could also maintain silence to the point of weirdness, making us all uneasy. In the midst of Jerry's pervasive minginess and repercussions of the Danes' disaster, Nick learned that his wife suddenly needed cancer tests, and he was a long way from home. We all felt he should leave and head home to her, but he felt so responsible for us, he wouldn't do it. Poor man. It threw everything off-center, trying to have a great time yet at the same time carry on.

Our motel, the Mercure, was close by. Pink Mediterranean walls beckoned through an arcade of palms and swaying bougainvillea. Inside, a patio revealed the sparkling blue of a clean, fresh swimming pool. And in it, doing its robotic cleanup, was a writhing, whimsical creepy crawler vacuum, slithering and coiling its tube maniacally about the pool—a crazy centerpiece.

There was revivifying coffee in the lobby; we helped ourselves, donned our suits, and had a nice dip. Afterward, lolling poolside and lulled by the mindless scuttling of the pool equipment, my eye was caught by vigorous rhythmic motions in a tree-shaded corner of the garden. What!

Youthful lovers were doing "it" right *there*. They finished their business and then rearranged themselves and left, smiling sweetly at us as they strolled past. I think I lost my aplomb. The men had been totally engrossed in conversation, and *gracias a Dios*, missed it. Busy little garden, what with them and the creepy crawler. I knew that open sex was *de rigueur* in the South Seas, but in Australia? This was getting thematic.

After dark, looking for the guys, Hal and I discovered the Front Pub, the Mercure's down-and-dirty pool hall—a place of tattoos, flip-flops or bare feet, and undershirts. Anything else, and they knew you were not one of them. An amiably curious young miner-type ambled over, glancing at our duds. "Hi, where yous from? America?"

"Why yes, how could you tell?" We grinned.

He advised that the other pub back inside the hotel would be more our type, where we'd find our mates. "You're a little old for this one." Ouch. But we had already checked over there for our group . . . No joy.

Here was noisy, barefoot, rock-and-roll, snockered pool—and what's this? A pretty old grizzled fella or two. Humph. We were too old, eh? Too nicey-nice, he meant. We gulped a VB and then skulked back to the less raucous hotel bar, found our pals, and waited. And waited . . . for the blue-hair tour to finish up. But the buffet was better than average, and they were not budging. That was okay— we used the time trying to top each other's jokes.

Port Hedland was a relatively new, rough mining town, said to be rowdy downtown. But the Mercure Inn on the outskirts was lovely, a pleasant stopping place in our travels. The moon turned the palm trees silver, reflecting a soft light into our walk back to our rooms. The night air was warm and soft.

Morning activities would again come early and soon. We had five hundred miles to cover the next day to Shark Bay with a fuel stop inland at Paraburdoo.

17 SHARK BAY

WHEN THE FIRST EUROPEAN farmers con-
fidently began to plant and irrigate crops with their effi-
cient old-world ways, they initiated an ecological disaster.
The water sucked up an underlying stratum of salt—whose
existence, naturally, was unknown to them. This formed
wonderfully strange patterns of salt-edged earth, like giant
paisleys, across the landscape. They finally figured they
would leave a tree in the middle of their clearings to keep
the water table under control. Ruination of the land, but
great visuals for us—especially in Western Australia.

"All stations Port Hedland, MBZ, Sierra Charlie
Uniform, tracking outbound 195 degrees at fifteen
hundred feet." Hal was at the helm, trading position information with an inbound aircraft from Paraburdoo, our
intended fuel stop. The day would bring a long haul over
huge expanses of dry desert. It was unfailingly, strangely
beautiful, rather like some of our western United States,
but the flavor was different—and it changed constantly.

PARABURDOO FUEL STOP

For this leg, we decided to navigate using the GPS for backup only—and, dismayed, found the VOR receiver (navigational aid used for guidance) disagreeing definitively with the GPS, as did the ADF . . . which performed perfectly on broadcast stations but not the NDBs (non-directional beacons)—those showed us consistently thirty degrees right of course. Egad. But maybe we had it wrong? Too ambiguous, too confusing. That was a mystery we never unwound. Never mind . . . We measured and timed ourselves according to the flight plan and found ourselves well on track and time to Paraburdoo (Aboriginal for "white cockatoo"). Winds were less favorable than forecast. What a surprise. We sighted our landmark, the giant Tom Pierce mine . . . it slid past on the right, and soon we spied our landing strip.

A pretty blonde refueled the planes, lighting up the ramp with happy smiles, recharging our good humor along with the gas tanks. After a quick soda break, off we roared into the wind, tracking for coastal Carnarvon. Long wavy ridgelines of shrubby dunes passed beneath us, some of them set about with curious clay and salt pans plopped across the landscape like giant oval polka dots. We flew along bemused by the patterns—of course they were quite infertile.

The winds then became so adverse we had to change course and skip some sightseeing, proceeding directly to Shark Bay to save time and fuel. Riveting blue waters, swirls of coral and sand—and then we were into Shark Bay's crosswind approach. Prewarned of a narrow runway, we were glad to find new improvements.

Shark Bay . . . A destination that would reveal remarkable oddities of nature, attracting people from far away. The airport manager was occupied with commercial operations, so we waited. And studied large swallow-like tawny golden kites wheel and soar on slender pointed wings, riding a useful rooftop ridge lift around the hangars. When done with his duties, he welcomed us warmly, confirmed our selected parking area as "just right," and wished us a fine stay.

OVAL PANS UP CLOSE and SNAFU

But soon, a snafu. Nick had been given flawed directions from the Heritage Resort contact who said it was "right next door to Monkey Mia." Totally, stupidly wrong. The cabbie intently drove twenty-four kilometers the wrong way through miles of lonesome scrub and big skies, until it was noted he was totally offtrack, and then he exasperatedly drove all the way back again and beyond, to the right place. A bright note—at our frustrated turning back at a crossroads, we got out to stretch our legs. No traffic, horizon to horizon. Wandering to the side, Nick spotted a wondrous little spiny creature, the almost invisible Australian horned lizard (thorny dragon or thorny devil) so hard to see for its earthy camouflaging.

And what else? Some of those surreal oval "pans" we had marveled at while airborne, odd amorphous lacy-edged shapes formed by dried salts, now appeared out in the landscape. A revelation. They were not even interesting at eye level. I can liken it to peering at Monet's *Water Lilies* from up close, seeing the brush strokes but losing the picture. Ground huggers have no idea what they're missing.

Denham's Heritage Resort was a modern, pleasant beach resort. After throwing our stuff into our rooms, we found its smoke-filled bar with a pool table. I threw myself into the scene . . . some beer-reeking guys, armed with cue sticks, cheerfully coached me. With sidelong looks at each other, they swore I'd be okay with practice. Oh sure.

Giving that up, Hal and I walked the beach promenade overlooking the sea and fell in with some Aussies staying at our hotel. They had once been pilots themselves and were intrigued by our flyabout. You could tell they wished they hadn't given it up. Maybe once you experience it, you never get over the need for the overview.

MONKEY MIA

In the morning we backtracked to Monkey Mia (say my-ya), a beach and ocean wilderness reserve where great stately pelicans slowly patrolled the sand, alternately still as statues, now and then moving serenely to groom themselves. Their eerie black, yellow-ringed, shoe-button eyes zeroed in on us (Hal said they looked like sewed-on doll's eyes). I wanted to read some reaction in there, but there was nothing, nothing, in those flat, bottomless eyes.

Not threatening, though—they just hoped for a nice fish.

STROMATOLITES

Gingerly, we waded into the surf along with a small group of other tourists. Friendly yet elusive dolphins drifted and fed among the throng of rolled-up pant legs. Being that close to these intelligent water mammals was extraordinary. Indoors we watched videos that explained the area, including up-close shots of this coastal location's unique oddities, its rare "live rocks"—scientific name stromatolites. Under the water, shallow, stratified limestone formations had living surfaces of microorganisms, layered with fossils of cyanobacteria. These peculiar growths were discovered here in this special area of high saline saturation in 1956—there are few other such clusters in the world.

TOO OLD TO FLY? MAYBE NOT . . .

During this month of exploration and discovery, I often thought of inquisitive, adventuresome old Phil, a man who loved to travel. He was a guy taking flying lessons when I took mine, a fellow in his late seventies. He took lessons, soloed successfully, but just couldn't study to pass the written exam to qualify for carrying passengers. Well, his wife didn't want to go up with him anyway, so he flew about without her on his renewable student solo license. This worked so well that when they traveled off to see the world, he would find a local airport, get a checkout from the rental place, rent an airplane, and have his solo sightseeing overview. Our flight school got postcards from exciting exotic places—like the highest airport in South America. He would have loved Shark Bay . . . he and his bride could have arrived commercially and then he could have rented a plane and seen for himself the sweeping coastlines of Western Australia . . . just his cup of tea. He showed me that anybody, so motivated, can learn—at any age.

There was also George . . . he was just sixty-five, freshly retired and freshly licensed, fulfilling a dream of his lifetime. But as a retiree, his funds became limited. So much so that his wife gave him an ultimatum: quit his nonsense and stop that flying. To be sure his wings were clipped, she allowed him only twenty-five dollars a week pin money. Poor George.

Hmm. That was just enough for a half hour of aircraft rental. Why didn't we split an hour of flying between us? We would fly someplace, land, and switch seats—one flying one way, the other navigating with the chart and then vice versa. I took him up to altitudes he'd not been to before to show him the grander overview, above scattered clouds dotting the landscape like so many sheep, so he could someday have some fun on his own. It was our and the flight school's secret. This practice continued until he navigated us to a wrong airport. The two airports had similar layouts—crossing runways between highways and a river and they were not all that far apart. Easy to confuse if you weren't on the correct heading . . . which we were not, thank you, George. The tower controller said, "There are showers in the northeast quadrant, and watch out for the airliner." Huh? Not where we were . . . egad and holy s--t, there came a plane climbing up on takeoff right at us as I was sliding down that same track on final to land. I jerked to the right, avoiding a head-on. Later I told George, "No more splitsies." It was my fault for not backstopping him. Nonetheless, the deal was off. Both of us had learned from it. Only one PIC (pilot in command) at a time.

Moral: Watch out!

I felt sad for George. I'd had flight training costs lightened by my enthusiastic father. He had been generous, understanding my passion, delighted to feed it till I was properly licensed. For advanced ratings, I negotiated a swap of aircraft use for airport office work—and then I became a glider tow pilot for a local glider club, free flying but for low-cost club fees. The club had a marvelous rule mandating that for every twenty tows the tow pilot had to get into the glider, taking a turn to experience the issues at the trailing end of the tow rope. Quickly I had enough flights to notch my belt with a glider rating.

Next day, on to Perth.

18 FLIGHT TO PERTH

THE DAY BROKE CLOUDLESS, assuring excellent weather for our next leg. After climbout, we turned out over the dazzling panorama of Denham Sound and its oddly named Useless Loop (the harbor was once believed blocked by sandbars, ergo useless)—and the Freycinet Estuary.

Headings and altitudes organized, all aircraft settled into a lovely coastal meander—abruptly Dixie (aircraft VHDXE) came up on frequency. Brad and Reggie were saying they did not have enough fuel to make Jandakot, Perth's satellite GA (general aviation) airport. (This airport outside of Perth was designated for smaller aircraft than the airlines, to keep them out of the way of the big boys.) No way could they stretch it. Lacking range in their tanks, pilot Reggie had fretted about their fuel supply before we even departed Shark Bay. Thoughtfully we flew along, casting our eyes over gypsum pans that morphed the landscape into a spectacular geological paisley.

Finally, the expected transmission. Yep—Nick announced a route change. We would track to Geraldton

for fuel top-offs. Good-sized Geraldton had a fitting airport for serving its large farming community. We headed
straight for it. Suddenly we soared out of the beige desert
into the verdant, sunny, west-coast farming area. What a
change. Rolling stretches of emerald green, fields of patch-
work purples, and vibrant yellow flowering crops . . . Never
had farms looked more beautiful. Aviation was a critical el-
ement in this remote agricultural area, and so the land was
rife with airstrips.

Something about "tail numbers"—the civil aviation
registration number assigned to individual aircraft, his-
torically found on the tail. The first is the country letter
designation. For example, ours was VHSCU. The VH indi-
cates Australian civil aircraft, N first on US airplanes, D for
Germany, JA for Japan, etc.) Early on, we playfully dubbed
(VH)DXE "Dixie." Our craft, SCU, was "Skoo." RPL would
be "Ripple," a shorthand that occasionally popped into
transmissions. Cessna 172 "Dixie" had the smallest tanks

and therefore the least range. Piper Cherokee 140 "Ripple" was the slowest, and our Cessna 172 "Skoo" was the fastest with its 180 horsepower Penn Yan engine conversion—although it had constraints placed on its range of operations. We enjoyed its speed advantage, but the operational limits were fuel consuming and annoying. We didn't mind the extra fuel stop.

Skoo's owner, Australian Jack Corrigan, had worked out a leaseback arrangement with Nick, which was good for us—a well-performing aircraft we were tickled to fly. Jack was a dashing entrepreneurial developer who loved fast living, the cravings for which later had sent him hard into a tree in a motorcycle race, ultimately shortening him by two inches. He was an Irish-descended Aussie we actually knew pretty well, he having been with us on our first trip into deepest Australia. Later he visited us in the United States to fly the New York City VFR corridor and circle the Statue of Liberty. He had also been with us at a memorable Oshkosh fly-in when, on the ground, an out-of-control aircraft ran hideously amuck, doing full-power S-turns through the tie-downs, dramatically and inconveniently smacking our parked plane along with four others. Another story.

So, Dixie needed a top-off. That gave us a chance to see what else lay below, even if it was just another airport. Well, it never is "just" another airport.

We had tootled through the sky at a high comfort level, knowing we wouldn't have to fixate on the gas gauge. Now, our bodies´ fuel was running low. Although Geraldton was purported to be an airport with commercial activity, alas it wasn't enough to warrant a nice little café. We got more gas, stocked up on vending machine junk, and then fired up again. Some arrogant Prussian type on final in a well-muscled twin engine didn't like where little DXE was running up preparing for takeoff—and he rudely lambasted him over the frequency. What was that about? It was all dirt, no marked hold lines—pilot's discretion on that most everywhere—and DXE was in no way a hazard. Besides, the Nazi was landing well down the runway. I bristled. What's German for "chicken shit"? "*Scheisskopf*" was close.

Never mind. Up and away on our coastal meander. Picture book white puffies had developed pretty fully over the land at around fifteen hundred feet, almost blotting out the bright blue with their flat gray bottoms. While we refueled, the ceiling had filled into a broken overcast that stretched way on out. Flying just underneath it to regain the shoreline, we then ranged beyond to parallel the landmass under clear ocean skies.

Another grand day of commanding seascapes. How will we ever come down to real life, away from all this faraway beauty? Ringed coral cays offshore, colorful rocky coastlines softened by pearly scalloped beaches, and the occasional picturesque harbor village. Reggie said those were shrimping and lobstering villages and that the infrequent shack on the shore was a hideout for folks skirting the law.

I believed anything Reggie said. He knew things.

THE PINNACLES

Along the airway to Perth came our next geological surprise. At Nambung National Park, an amazing display of extraordinary "Pinnacles" stretched nearly horizon to horizon. Hundreds of limestone extrusions arose below us, straight up from the miles-wide flat surface, standing erect as sentinels, ranging from a foot to a few meters tall. They took on the hue of the land where they extruded from the earth, yellow, ochre, or gray. Hal and I strayed a bit from the group to swing low in slow flight for a closer look. Flaps out, engine back to 1600 rpm, three hundred feet, ambling along in the air ... We don't have anything like them in the United States. (I muttered those words often. When it seemed we'd seen it all—another curiosity would surface.) We didn't dare blink. But an interesting note—when I have looked for reference pictures of the Pinnacles, they are always beige-gray. We had the advantage of going to where there are no roads and saw more curious colors and beauty.

As we had swooped down slowly for the Pinnacles perusals, I was jogged into memories of another slow flight, many years before, in my first little airplane, a 1959 Cessna 172 with flaps that operated the old way, by a hand lever. Simply put, flaps control the downward angle of the nose so you can go slower and see down and forward better. The added square feet of wing brought by lowered flaps add more lift while at the same time slowing you down. Useful for landings. That flight had puttered up a winding valley creek in Vermont, carrying a friend's father eager for a scenic (nosy) tour past his nephew's cabin and then roaring upward to peer into a lady friend's bedroom as she enjoyed her morning coffee. I'll never forget her face as she jerked erect to the sight of an airplane cruising over her lawn with a wing-waggle "hello." That was old-timey hedgehopping at its best—in America's own kind of outback, the Northeast Kingdom. I had picked up my passenger at the "Tater Hill" grass airstrip on the lumpy hillside of a little country club carved out of the woodlands. Sweet. So rural, so rustic. Most importantly, so sparsely populated. There are regulations describing altitude restrictions over thickly settled areas. My dear old friend, Nancy Hopkins Tier (God rest her soul), had as a young woman buzzed Hoover's inaugural parade, causing the feds to make some rules.

And so here in Australia we sped on along the track—destination, Perth.

PERTH ARRIVAL, JANDAKOT AIRPORT

SCU (me): "Jandakot Tower," (call-in from checkpoint Katherine, a distinct town from the air), "Cessna 172, Sierra Charlie Uniform, approaching Katherine at fifteen hundred feet inbound with Delta." (Transcribed airport information available on discrete frequencies is given a letter designation from the international phonetic alphabet).

Controller: "Roger, Sierra Charlie Uniform, will you be

coming by Adventure?" Good heavens, how did he know? Oh funny—of course that was the name of the lake resort checkpoint on our inbound route. (In case you are from another planet and don't know what "roger" means, it means "transmission received and understood.")

SCU: "Affirmative, Jandakot . . . Sierra Charlie Uniform is coming in via Adventure."

He advised me to proceed and join runway twenty-four right (there was also a twenty-four left) on its downwind.

Downwind? Explanation . . . you can skip this if you want.

Upwind, Downwind, Crosswind, Base, Final. Names for the sides of the invisible overhead rectangular pattern boxing the runway in the air, a path usually flown around the runway before you land. It helps orient you to the runway and its final approach to your safe landing—at any airport. The pattern is useful in joining the possible stream of aircraft coming in to land on your and their destination runway.

Upwind parallels the side of the strip with the wind direction coming at you. The upwind parallels the final approach descent line to the landing. An upwind is often used when coming in to join the landing pattern from another area.

Crosswind is the line or side of the rectangle used to cross over to the other side of the runway from the upwind line—across the wind, as it were—from which one subsequently turns onto the . . .

Downwind leg has the following wind, or wind pushing you along, into which you will eventually be facing for the landing.

Base leg is the base line of the rectangle, the line or side to fly to join up with the . . .

Final approach—the final descent to your touchdown place . . . into the headwind again as it was also on the upwind side. One flies into a headwind to slow the landing speed, the wind pushing against the forward progress of the plane.

A few more brief confirming exchanges with the Jandakot tower controller, and we were down, rolling off onto the taxiway. The fun began.

Wherever was Bernie's? Bernie's, the place where we were to tie ourselves down.

We began a timid prowl through crowded taxiways, wandering helplessly through a large hangar complex. No directions from ground control . . . out of his range of radio communication. We were on our own. Someone volunteered that it was "over there by the Royal Flying Doctor's Hangar." But no, it wasn't. I paused and queried a bearded local who grinned and offered, "Park here at my place," until he learned we were a trio of planes. He didn't have that much room. "Bernie's is wa-a-a-y down that way— take the taxiway between the last hangars and look for *gibble-gabble-gibble*," (something unintelligible to our Yankee ears). "Bernie's name isn't actually on the building yet." Oh boy.

Befuddled, we taxied "wa-a-a-y down that way," and then shut the plane down to ask another somebody in a hangar about Bernie's. Opaque instructions. We gave up and moved the plane off the taxiway onto some handy grass. "Why not?" I muttered to myself. Why do I always get this job? Hal says I can chat up strangers better than he can.

Yeah, yeah. Here, I was nervously uneasy. I dreaded doing a "wrong thing" in our leader's eyes since he had revealed himself as being unapologetically macho.

In a moment along came the others . . . I was pop-eyed, watching them taxi to us, pull up—and park. Whaddya know . . . Danged if we hadn't ended up right outside of Bernie's. My relief was overwhelming, but never would I show it. Would I tell anyone it was sheer luck that we found it? Moi? Not.

The van arrived. A little small for us six, with all our bags. But the driver wedged us in and carefully packed our bags around our bodies. "You'll all fit," he said . . . "No wasted spaces."

Bad idea. Very bad.

"Ladies first," he had said. So I was first to clamber in. Uh-oh. That meant the backseat, stuffed into that dead-air backseat, getting sweaty. All of a sudden, in a rising tsunami of claustrophobia that hit ka-pow to my psyche, in a spectacularly fast reflex I catapulted forward to front seat relief—so fast no one knew what was happening. I still can see Reggie's surprised face as I whizzed over him.

Up front could have been the best seat in the house. But—our burly chauffeur was expat Polish and felt it most important to bore us with his version of what was wrong with Australia. Yawn. When he realized he had Americans on board, he announced that his dad, in the sixties, had been the Polish ambassador to the United States. Really? You think?

But it's a weird world. Maybe he was.

From Jandakot's location well south of town, all the way to our downtown digs, we rumbled an hour through urban traffic to the tune of his tiresome tirade. Made the stuffy backseat look good.

Relief came with the Chateau Commodore, a nice, city-kind of hotel. Right in the center, around the corner from Symphony Hall. We registered, found our rooms, and gleefully noted that, like all nice city hotels, it importantly offered laundry and dry cleaning. With no organized tour schedule, our group split up to go separate ways for the next two days, following our own devices. That night for dinner Hal and I skipped the pubs, opting for more opulence. Our boys later reported that they had done "Freo," Fremantle, and some of its fine pubs.

That evening, SCU's crew dined in elegance at Il Campo de Fiori restaurant in East Perth, where the waiters rushed, but we didn't. A fine bottle of Fermoy Cabernet Sauvignon 1992 and all the culinary accoutrements set us right for the later luxury of a comfy hotel bed and as much time as we wanted in it.

There was that symphony hall . . . Maybe a concert? Did I mention how cosmopolitan Perth is?

19 PERTH, SECOND DAY

NO EARLY RISING, A universally appreciated moment in travelers' lives. But stretching blissfully, we realized we actually wanted to get up and at 'em anyway. Weeks of habit. We met the others at breakfast, but we were going to rent a car and roam down the coastline toward the famed Margaret River wineries, and they had their plans. We were hyped up to check out this huge city and its countryside, a metropolis so far from home. How did city people here live, work, and play? Like others of their ilk, no doubt.

Motoring along, we noted that the highway had its own flavor. Though quite like our interstates, you knew you were elsewhere. A particular billboard greeted our eyes: "WE DON'T PLAY ANY MUSIC WITH 'YO' IN IT!" Oh *yessss*. Our kind of country. We veered off onto side roads to go roaming.

COWS and CALLAS

We became so besotted with the byroads that the Margaret River plan quickly collapsed. It was spring, and incredibly, stunningly lovely. Great bunches of calla lilies burgeoned in the gooey mud of damp cattle paddocks—growing elegantly in cattle muck? Hefty beef plodded and mooed uninterestedly among the lush clumps. Roadside verges passed by, thickly carpeted with yellow blossoms of all shades. And perky bluebonnets, and pink ice plants . . . And huge golden gorse, extraordinary coral banksias, and waving golden yellow wattle.

Wattle? What is a wattle, I mused? Happily here it's a genus of acacia, the floral symbol of Australia, not a fleshy fold around the neck.

I thought back on glorious long-ago California spring-times, before housing grids, those mountain-to-seaside developments that effectively eradicated its open fields and wild woods. Back in the days when its soft low hills were painted with a dancing prism of golden poppies, Indian paintbrush, bluebonnets, buttercups, and wine cups, when drives down country roads were joyful staples of the passing of seasons, on roads that wound lazily among the hills so you could see it all. Now gone.

BIRDS: KOOKABURRA TO CURRAWONG

And then there were Australia's extraordinary warbling birds. You haven't experienced birdsong until you've heard it in Australia. Birds' trilling is not only decibels louder—it has character . . . the whipbird's call sounds exactly like a whizzing cracking bull whip; the many-voiced mimic lyrebird—graceful tail fashioned like a lyre—can sound like a magpie or a chainsaw; and the laughing kookaburra does indeed "laugh"—to name a few. They were swooping and darting—black and white magpies spilling liquid songs,

melodious currawongs, and flamboyant lorikeets squawk-
ing along with pink galahs, the parrot that plays the role of
our pigeons—except for the cooing. The galah is Australia's
ubiquitous line-sitter and airport hazard.

We passed through a cloudburst or two, splattering the
green serenity. Along the seashore we spied a mammoth,
towering, remote coastal loading facility, a ship lying at berth
beside the dock. There was some vigorous action around
it—grain cargo? Moving on, we dodged off track through a
village to discover sweetly quaint old-world architecture and
then wended on south, pottering happily to Bunbury. There
we sought out a café and continued to be impressed with
how well Australians know how to eat and cook.

Emerging contentedly from lunch, we stepped into a
rogue shower. Sunlight was suddenly blotted up in shadows
with a quick swirl of pelting raindrops—we ducked into a
bookstore. A tome on Australian humor met our eyes and
an irresistible wildflower compendium to add to the aircraft's heft. And then, oh good, next door a computer store.

For a fee, they would print out my daily log, my journal.
That was one of my outing goals . . . sometimes you just
need real paper in your hands for viewing and revising the
opus. Ah, but unfortunately, when the store's techno-geek
got hold of my laptop—whoosh!—he lost the entire cherished log. Vanished!

Just like that. My God. I went into a high-speed wobble,
muttering exclamatory disbelieving oaths at his rapidly
disappearing figure.

The coward turned his back on his dreadful ineptitude
and furtively slunk away, skulking into the employee-only
backroom—abandoning me to scan through all my files,

clammy-palmed with panic. Jerk! Folder by folder, with shaky fingers I desperately searched. Well, well . . . who'd have thought it? There it was! With the *Internet server*. Good grief. While "dragging" the file, pseudogeek hadn't been paying attention, and it slipped and whisked away from the mouse. But—the drama was done and over; such unspeakable relief. It was a rapidly spun kerfuffle, but terrifyingly slo-mo at the time.

By the inland route, we drove unhurriedly back to Perth and the Commodore on forested roads of handsome giant trees.

Referred by our hotel staff to first-class Italian fare at popular De Ricco's, we headed out to Subiaco, a gentrified upscale part of Perth. The Italian open-fire oven restaurant was packed with the chicly garbed, smacking their lips over marinaras and antipastos. And oh, the tender pastas, redolent with rich mouthwatering sauces. Having called ahead, we were seated quickly. The waiter immediately whisked into place a thoughtful saucer of herbed olive oil for sopping warm fresh crusty bread. The menu was complete . . . we had succulent veal and fish, prepared à la De Ricco. Later, after other customers had departed into the night, we lingered. Owner De Ricco himself joined us for a convivial moment or two, conversing enthusiastically about recipes and restaurants in faraway places. Having fully enjoyed his best and toasted each other several times, we bid smiling farewells and wound our way through dark city streets to our comfy beds. Closing happy tired eyes on that exceptional day we wondered—what would tomorrow bring?

Did I mention how cosmopolitan Perth is? But no concert—not yet.

20 PERTH III

TODAY WE WOULD PURSUE the concert idea. First, a morning consult with the concert hall receptionist, just down the street and around the corner. Liking our enthusiasm, she promised she would sneak us into the rehearsal that afternoon, after we accomplished our planned Kings Park outing.

KINGS PARK

We quickly motored up to the highest point in the city, to Perth's famous Kings Park—by now comfortable with left-side driving. These botanical gardens rank among the world's best, a landmark attraction spread out atop the city's most prominent hill. We perused lush plantings for a few pleasant hours, unraveling Latin names, and matching up specimens with what we'd seen at roadside—such as the bizarre and colorful "kangaroo paw"—and identifying indigenous birds by birdsong. Besides the common magpie and currawong, a little honeyeater was loudly trilling a

Johnny-one-note clarion bell chime. Under a giant spreading tree, *Toad of Toad Hall*, a play adapted from the endearing children's book *The Wind in the Willow,* was rehearsing. Our daughter had played in that at her antipodal Massachusetts high school. It was surprising to find Australian actors performing it here on the other side of the world, gamboling on a grassy greensward—a huge *de facto* stage with distant views of the city below.

Lunchtime! And good news, right here in the park was Fraser's, one of Perth's most outstanding restaurants. What bliss. Where else on earth can you roll *haute cuisine* around on your tongue, watch warbling honeyeaters sipping from blossoms, and get a smashing city view *al fresco*, alongside perhaps the most splendid giant eucalyptus in the entire world?

At the gift shop we picked up a handsome little hand-carved box for Hal, plus some postcards—and then it began to rain.

FREMANTLE

Dodging fat raindrops, we scurried to the car and dashed to Fremantle, a resurrected and now-upscale seaside area full of its own brand of picturesque residential architecture—and the notorious Fremantle Gaol, the 1800s convict-built prison. It shut down forever in 1991, shortly before our trip to Perth, and was designated a UNESCO World Heritage Site and museum. We took a peek, but prisons are prisons with grim threads in common. No need to dwell on it.

We poked about Fremantle's streets, stopped for ice cream, and headed back home to the open rehearsal. Busy day.

Concert Hall—its acoustics were superb, its appearance elegantly handsome, the seats better than concert-hall comfortable—and we got to hear a new clever and inspired composition called "Strung Out," by a local composer, Roger Smalley. There were thirteen musicians strung out across the stage playing strings. We could have settled in for the whole piece, but we had bought tickets for that evening's performance.

The full performance later was outstanding, although our assigned seats were under a sound-dampening balcony. Hal growled, "How disconcerting," and acknowledged his pun was the lowest form of humor but he couldn't help it. So annoying, that muffling you get under the overhang. At the interval, chatting with musicians, Hal, always the businessman, started digging into the economics of the Perth Concert Hall. They explained that it had been built by the city with help from state and national governments and managed by the Perth Theatre Trust. Smalley's creation couldn't have had a better venue . . . Intermission over, we shifted to empty center seats and better acoustics for a many-voiced romantic Poulenc organ concerto.

After that, Beethoven's Second—never heard it done better. During the intermission we also learned the West Australian Symphony Orchestra is a daily rehearsed, full-time endeavor, totally supported by state and business benefactors. No wonder it was first class.

We slipped out of the concert early, rushing to a dinner booking at the strangely named, highly acclaimed "The Loose Box." (Yes, I know. Keep your thoughts to yourself.)

LOOSE BOX INN

The Loose Box Inn restaurant, its French chef hired from Bordeaux, was said to be one of the best in the area—but it was a long wild drive up into the hills into Mundaring. A destination restaurant née farmhouse with essential country charm, its dining room ell had been part of some renovated stables, later moved here for creative reuse. How? That provocative name "loose box" refers to a movable horse stall. The prices were steep and almost worth it. "Hmm," we said to each other. What's this delicacy? Yabbies? To demo, they brought out a little live crayfish clicking around on a plate, bravely brandishing his tiny fierce claws in futile defense. After that, we just couldn't. He was so endearing.

Our waiter was newly arrived from South Africa, a flight instructor supporting his family until he could get his credentials validated in Australia. We spoke about the annual World Precision Flying Championship held in Fort Worth, where we had recently been judges—South African pilots had been there to compete. It's a small aviation community in South Africa, and sure enough, he knew them.

We sped back through the night, yawning against sleep, glad we had not missed this distinctive place.

Or anything else about cosmopolitan Perth.

AUSSIES ARE NICKNAMED "DIGGERS"

Having gone down the western coast of Australia, the next day we would start flying eastward again to the gold mining town of Kalgoorlie. If it were anything like Tennant Creek, a little outback mining town we visited another year, I would be mighty disillusioned. That primitive gold mine, though interestingly antique and reeking of history, was so small, old, and constrictive I could not bring myself to ease into the one-person-wide tight descent. Not on my to-do list, wriggling, squeezing down a rickety ladder into dark tunnels, scuffing elbows and backside on chiseled-out walls. There I had settled for billy tea and waited above at the campfire.

21 To Kalgoorlie

We met at early breakfast to group up for departure for Kalgoorlie—the site of the great Kalgoorlie gold mining project that young engineer Herbert Hoover had been involved in before his tenure as US President. Gold? In the middle of a huge desert wilderness? How did they ever find it? What called them to that place? I guess in sniffing for gold, people scrabble about until they finally hit pay dirt—or not. By now I was tuned to the fact that this mine was no little Tennant Creek-style old-time dig.

Reggie and Brad, in miserable shape after some bad "dogs eyes" (meat pies) in Freo, could barely muster themselves. They looked greenish and felt awful. The sky over downtown Perth was dazzling blue, but when we got to outlying Jandakot, we found the airport gray and misty in low IMC (instrument conditions in low clouds and fog). We were grounded until the weather lifted. So we paced around, sat around, and poked into hangars to see what was what. In one, they were piecing together new Bellanca airplanes from the United States, shipped in parts. Out on the grass, we desultorily stirred up black-crested cockatoos that were flocking and pecking, starling-like, and then we chatted up the Beechcraft dealer. And waited. The waiting was good for Brad and Reggie.

Jandakot has a departure procedure to follow when conditions improve enough to become Special VFR (one thousand feet ceiling and three miles visibility). VFR pilots are then permitted to leave, should they wish to. The weather for SVFR isn't all that great, but it's good enough to kind of see your way around. So when clouds lifted a bit and the visibility improved, cleared by air traffic control, we took off, climbing quickly to scoot out under the low ceiling. Peering about for oncoming traffic, we crossed over green hills and fields to clear skies and dry lands. At those SVFR altitudes in such a narrow corridor you're likely to about skin somebody coming the other way—and we nearly did. I can still see him now, popping out of the murk . . . a low-wing type. We passed each other whizzing fast and close, keeping to our designated sides of the corridor. At home we'd have called it a "near miss."

GOLD, GOLD DIGGERS, and HISTORICAL WHORES

So on to Kalgoorlie, the richest gold-saturated square mile in the world. With the biggest gold mine in the world, Kalgoorlie's mine defines the word "enormous." Its ore trucks, the megabehemoths of all trucks, haul a kajillion tons. But they're dwarfed to ant size in the wide, massive "pit," the nickname for the mine. Approaching by air, you'd expect jerry-built tacky town here . . . but no. Handsome, substantial, late Victorian and early Edwardian buildings lined the wide main street, colorfully painted to enhance

 the architecture, the town full of excellent renovations and restorations. Overhangs reached out beyond storefronts to shade sidewalks against the searing sun, and the sidewalks bustled with people.

Aborigines were there in the background, as always, in the corners of the outdoors. They sullenly kept their own company, squatting and sitting around on the ground in clumps. Primitive outsiders in nearly every way. They must really seethe at their lot. They looked like they do. There seemed to be an invisible wall that I dared not try to broach, even for a passing greeting—and surely not idle chitchat.

Colorful pubs dotted the wide Main Street, wide windows open to lure in the thirsty. These were interspersed with period hotels, the old covered marketplace, and town buildings. Ankle-challenging deep V-gutters rimmed the thoroughfares for flash rain runoffs—we quickly learned to be wary. It's an old desert town lacking some sophistication but with up-to-date merchandise. A nice mix. Our cab driver told us that because of available construction jobs, the town had grown terrifically and become yuppified. Lots of restorations, many new developments. The modern mining museum was a well-conceived window on Kalgoorlie's past, from antique battered mining tools and horrifying old dental equipment—even to, oh my goodness—long time ago Buy-Five-Get-One-Free hooker tokens.

Hookers? Oh yessss.

As it happened, behind Main Street was Hay Street, the historical infamous brothel row . . . still in operation, though not as heavily used, I think. Curiosity drew us there after dinner. We sloped along self-consciously in a loose line, slack-jawed with amazement. Porn-packaged vamps solicited closely from sidewalk-level copulation cubbies, tarted up, seamy, and sleazy. Creepy. One hopeful whore reached out and stroked Hal's arm in invitation. Yikes! He

was as off-put as I was. I'm not sure, but I may have hissed, "Get your dirty hands off my man!" We all sensed the griminess of it and moved on quickly. In the olden days there was a five-hundred-to-one ratio of miners to prostitutes and thirty thousand miners! *Oof.* I guess satisfying male needs cut way back on high-testosterone fights. Today the slutty vendors are still available, the current batch of prostitutes ostensibly there for the randy lonely men in town—although the numbers of needy miners have diminished greatly, modern mining equipment having put so many diggers out of a job. This raunchy moneymaking activity is still permitted in modern times because, well, Hay Street is *historic.* (Yeah, sure.)

Our chic, gleaming chrome, glass, and polished wood dinner restaurant was brand new, open less than ten days. Its organizers hadn't quite shaken out the fine details . . . the local-talent waitress simpered and said, "Umm, we have specials but I forget what they are," grinning enchantingly—or so she thought. Our boys were too hungry to be charmed.

Brad was about to rip his dinner out of the kitchen, it took so maddeningly long. But by the time the place abruptly went dark in a power failure, we had been fed and didn't mind. It seemed properly atmospheric and fitting for an old mining town. We lingered companionably on the sheltered terrace in the sweet night air, mildly interested as an electrician dug around in the wall beside us. He righted some wiring glitch, and the restaurant's bustling pace resumed. The owners were from Perth and planned it to be very Fremantle, in keeping with Kalgoorlie's apparent trend as an oasis in the middle of nowhere.

Ansett Australia ran a big business crowd into town and out every morning and afternoon through the new airy glass and steel airport terminal. But except for the odd charter, the terminal was dead empty in between those two flights. Surely someday there will be more. Or maybe fewer, when the ore runs out. There was nothing else but tourism to support the town. Well, that works for many places, doesn't it?

And then there's always Hay Street.

22 THE NULLARBOR

Next stop, WA/SA. But first a takeoff over the astounding pit, with a chance to marvel again at its extreme size and twist around to watch it vanish into the hazy horizon. We climbed to nine thousand feet for cooler outside temperatures and turned our minds to navigating. Basically, we just followed a heading and a railroad. It was that simple, over the Nullarbor.

Say Null-ah-bore, accent on the first syllable. The Nullarbor Plain, a place with no trees. No arbor . . . Catchy. Once it was a sheep-raising area, but no more. I would blame the bare lands on those close-munching sheep, razing the grass right to the dirt, but the real culprit is no doubt the dearth of rain.

The vast Nullarbor lies south of the Great Victoria Desert, and just farther up that snugs against the Gibson Desert, and then the far northern Great Sandy Desert unrolls as you work your way finally toward the Kimberley—the Kimberley, where we enjoyed Taffy's shady Mount Hart respite and Sarah's good cooking. A lot of extremely hostile beauty for a few thousand miles, one end of Australia to the other.

The enormous dry outback . . . and this is Western Australia's version of it, here at the southern coast.

Once, aloft at seven thousand feet with an instructor—a man who had logged an impressive twenty thousand hours of flight—he turned to me beaming and said, "Aren't we lucky? Up here like this? All those goggle-eyed ground huggers down there haven't a clue how wonderful this is." He still loved that overview, after all those years. Me too, especially here.

And so it was . . . The arresting 360-degree panorama so immense and stark, nature's mottled gray and rusty red artwork with a straight-as-a-string horizon as far as we could see from ninety-five hundred feet above it. The land was inscribed with red clay pans and "tanks" (watering holes), animal tracks leading to their evaporating centers, looking from far above like so many ganglia—and interesting swirls of stubby spinifex brush that grow in the round and then die in the center, forming intriguing rings.

Ruler-straight railroad tracks extended for hundreds of miles across the arid landscape, disappearing sometimes into the hazy distance, and so we eventually came to the lonesome small settlement of Forrest.

What's this? A cluster of maintenance trucks were on the tracks at a singularly isolated intersection—we riveted on the action. The crossing seemed to be the only one for as far as the eye could see. How curious . . . so few signs of humanity. Later that evening at our WA/SA stop, way beyond Forrest, we caught a snippet of TV coverage of a terrible collision that had happened there during the night. So remote . . . figure the odds. How could anyone not notice a speeding train, lights flashing, whistle blowing—

and get whacked? So few trains, so few cars. Suicide? Bad luck for that engineer. So strange, our happening upon the accident's grim cleanup.

After Forrest, the route swung southeast to our night's destination Border Village Motel, at WA/SA, the Western Australia/South Australia state border on the coast. By road, it's five hundred miles in one direction to a post office and nine hundred miles in the other direction to another. We had come from one end and were going to the other. Puttering in for the dirt-strip landing at the motel, we tied down and off-loaded our bags. Being in such a remote rustic area, the motel turned out to be the most you could hope for: clean and neat with decent food—and a handy pub.

23 WA/SA

REMOTE? TALK ABOUT TIMBUKTU. Border Village in the Nullarbor was smack on the state line of Western Australia and Southern Australia (WA/SA), isolated and surreally remote. Mail and newspapers came in only twice a week—when a bus passed through. It was just inland from the Great Australian Bight on one of the most stunning stretches of coastline in the world. This section of the continent rises from the sea for hundreds of miles as one long vertical cliff, a sheer three-hundred-foot cliff carved by eons of wave action. This geological feature goes on and on, vanishing into distant faint haze. It's here that UFO sightings proliferate. Or did. It's said that Air Force pilots would come roaring in across the sea at night, aircraft landing lights full on, heading straight at the bluffs in their P-3 Orions and then they would cut their engines for some silent mischief, converting forward speed and inertia into a fast pull-up, hurtle over those cliffs, and then silently level off. When their airspeed dropped, they would fire up again—just before they ran out of momentum—and whiz off into the distant nighttime. Locals were adamant in their belief that aliens were right here. They had seen their spaceship lights. It was even reported in the area newspapers from time to time.

The Border Village Motel. What an enterprise in such an impressively large and desolate place on our globe. A large part of the region is protected, named the Eucla (a settlement farther along down the coast) and Nullarbor Wilderness. Good we landed in the Dry—during rainy periods the dirt strip becomes greasy and slippery in mud. I'll take a dusty pebble-dinged prop to one pranged by sliding off the runway any day. A couple of adventuring Texans nearly did that—the dirt strip was so gooey in the Wet, their chosen time to tour. Scared them big time. En route back home, our Qantas pilot pulled a news write-up from his wallet, a clipping sent to him by that couple. They almost got themselves marooned. Stuck at WA/SA with a broken plane? Don't even think it.

DIRT STRIPS

In the United States, we don't see many dirt strips. Most airstrips are paved these days or are lovely grass runways, nicely tended. But there were places . . .

Decades ago, a five-town area of central Massachusetts had been sacrificed for the greater good . . . the whole valley was flooded so that Boston could have a better water supply. Well, when dry spells came along and the reservoir's level dropped enough, old roads surfaced—two of them made excellent landing strips, remote and isolated from any civilization, detached from former road networks. I landed there myself, for the heck of it, even though it was rumored to be off-limits, FAA-wise. Hey—I never saw any paper that said that! Everybody did who could. And so, frisky youth would have its will be done, and legend has it that the odd fly-in coed picnics happened on one particularly nice road—with skinny-dipping. The word spread and gleeful mischief too. One joyful afternoon, interlopers snuck in on a canoe and whisked away the unattended clothes, leaving the partyers with sunburned bosoms and behinds, flummoxed and hopping wild with fury and angst. Nothing to be done. They had to fly back en deshabillé and explain things. The tale is still passed down, pilot to pilot. Those waters are looked on now either with raised eyebrows—or with happy, misty nostalgia. Or envy?

The Border Village itself was basically just a truck stop. A huge plaster kangaroo loomed up beside the highway with a Coca-Cola stubby in its paw, next to a giant ROAD-HOUSE sign. There was a pest control inspection station for vehicles to pass through before continuing east or west. Jerry, Hal, and I walked around and took pictures of each other beside these things, and waved toodle-oo to Reggie and Brad as they strode off resolutely toward where they figured there would of course be a beach. Hal sniffed and bet they wouldn't make it. Hal was right. They ended up running out of both roadway and path. They were not happy.

I chewed over the idea of the five-kilometer walk to the ocean outlook, thought better of it, and looked inside for someone to hire to drive me to the bluffs. Didn't want to miss my one chance to see the Indian Ocean with my own eyes with my feet on the ground. It turned out that Shona, a worker there, was willing. Hal wasn't about to be left behind—so off we motored with Shona's pet Pomeranian, Pepper, hopping from lap to lap. Bumping and rocking along, Shona gingerly coaxed her sedan of a certain creaking maturity down a rock-strewn road to the mother of all breathtaking precipices.

It was three hundred feet down to a creamy sandy beach—no access from our prospect. And no guard rails. This is wilderness, not park. It made our palms sweat being so near the edge, peering down at crashing waves. Plummeting death possibilities were right up there. Not the kind of place where you want to dangle your feet over the edge. But I began musing, how far from here was the Philippine Island of Luzon? And the South China Sea . . .

"KISS ME ONCE AND KISS ME TWICE, THEN KISS ME ONCE AGAIN, IT'S BEEN A LONG, LONG TIME"

When I was eight years old, my dad, amused by a daughter too antsy for tea sets, called me down from trees and rooftops and gave his tomboy daughter her first flight. Right after the end of World War II, we were at his wartime post, Floridablanca, on Luzon in the Philippines. To join him after war's end, my mother and I were shipped for twenty-one days on an army transport, across the Pacific from San Francisco, marveling at whale spouts and flying fish and riding out a pitching, rolling storm. We kids loved that, our own seagoing roller coaster. Most of the adults strapped themselves onto their bunks, retching. And oh, how the ship went wild at the equator crossing . . . sailors merrily chased after the prettiest women to deliver the traditional spanking! Lots of gasping and giggling . . . a happy riotous occasion. I wonder if they still do that, the equator crossing ritual. Probably not. Sexual harassment and all that. Pity.

A three-day layover in Okinawa. Postwar reconstruction. Raw and ugly. The land was in transition from war-torn to regreening, torn up by tractors and front-end loaders, clearing out bombed-out debris and landmines. Crowds of dark-eyed worker-natives stared at us pale Americans, me a blonde child, Mama and I wearing stylish mother-daughter flowered hat brims—no crowns. They had to think we were crazy. Hats were for shielding brains from a pounding sun.

A few days later our passage was done. We pulled in to dock at destination Manila. A brass band played with great gusto and feeling, "It's Been a Long, Long Time." We pressed against the railing, eagerly scanning the crowd, the pier so full of army caps, shouting and waving. The arriving dependents were busy spotting husbands and fathers, the men anxiously peering up to find sweethearts and children. I spied mine right away, intense and handsome, his face joyful at seeing us. Off the ship we rushed into his welcoming arms. I was surprised . . . a few little guys were quite terrified by these men their mommies were hugging—they hadn't seen them in so long that they didn't recognize them! Probably they had been babes in arms at their last encounter. Or waiting to hatch?

So there I was, sitting behind my pilot dad, riding over the South China Sea out of Luzon in a rackety single-engine reconnaissance plane with tandem seating. We ventured out to see the relics of his war, a few sunken warship hulks pointing their dead black hulls from sea to sky . . . I said how huge they were. Dad growled, "You should see the parts underwater." I was so young—but he must have wanted me to see that—and to remember.

Now I'm many years away from that flight. But how far away really was that Luzon bay on the South China Sea from this Indian Ocean now at my feet? Years and years back—but not so many nautical miles, both being part of the same vast far eastern sea. Across Australia and up the archipelago a bit, and Bob's your uncle, there's that bay. I wondered if those hulks were still there.

Shona was a pretty and warm New Zealander who came to Australia to get away from big stress. We sat and communed with the sea for a while and exchanged data. Back at the motel she showed us her exquisite handmade quilts. It came out that recently her daughter had died, and she was trying to make peace with that. We understood too well—we were using this trip to orbit ourselves away from the cancer death of our son. Not that it's possible, really, to do that, but changes of scenery are helpful. (See footnote at end of book.)

GOD MUST LOVE PILOTS BEST

A few years before, I had flown my teenager around on a college search, visiting a few down south that he thought he'd like to look at. We checked out two in Virginia, one in San Antonio—and then New Orleans Tulane University. That particular steamy Louisiana afternoon, the skies opened up with a magnificent Gulf Coast deluge, forcing us into a handy doorway, one that opened into delightful aromas of platters of boiled shrimp, bowls of gumbo, and mouth-watering po'boys. We feasted, the rain dried up, and we grabbed transport to the airport. I filed an instrument flight plan and then hopping over ramp puddles we climbed aboard our Cessna. I tuned in the ATIS (Automatic Terminal Information Service), received our clearance from ground control, and taxied out to the runway. The tower cleared us for takeoff—and off we climbed. Our bird rose through stunningly beautiful dappled cumulus, up through sunlit silvered cloud canyons toward brilliant blue, popping out on top of the ceiling . . . My averred agnostic son's eyes widened with wonder and delight, and he exclaimed, "Oh wow, God must really love pilots best!" Smiling, I said I believed he must.

THE WA/SA DESALINIZATION PLANT

First point of interest: the motel had its own desalinization unit. All the good drinking and bath water was processed from ocean water pumped up from the nearby ocean—just a short hop down the dirt path. We got the tour and technical description of the reverse-osmotic process by which it worked. Surprisingly simple, and a boon to this hot, miserably dried-out place. Rains that come during the Wet are not enough to store up for the rest of the year. Although an initially expensive installation, it was clearly the only remedy for total desiccation and a huge help to wayfarers. An obvious requirement for the motel, better than trucking in freshwater from afar.

Second point of interest: a twin Cessna 337, the kind with an engine in front to pull and one in back to push (whimsically known as a "push-me/pull-you"), arrived with a whale research veterinarian. Their plan was to fly up the Bight to check out the *Eubalaena australis*, the southern right whale. Here are its breeding grounds, areas where one finds pods seemingly without number. The chatty vet was almost vibrating with anticipation.

Waiting for our lunch, we amused ourselves in the dining room, people watching. Some odd creatures wandered in, raggedly dressed, dirty and dreadlocked . . . as if homeless. Hadn't seen this type since the smelly bathless hippie days of the United States. But no. Not homeless. Not exactly. I think they were traveling in an outfitted bus. "Ferals" Nick called them, jobless and irresponsible drifting young people with little drippy-nosed, unwashed kids they

fed only french fries, the entire gang garbed in pseudome-
dieval dress. He felt they should be reported. Me too, seeing
such neglect. Such odd role-playing, dressed in ratty knave-
and-serf clothing.

There were the usual bearded truckers as well, plus a
few touring retirees. But it was the usual theme: a long way
from anything in the middle of nowhere.

Our cabin was clean, the water good. That desalinization doodad worked just fine.

But I was looking forward to getting on with it.

24 To Ceduna, Wending Eastward

It was a sunny, blustery takeoff from WA/SA.

Wait a minute . . . you want to know blustery? I'll tell you about blustery. Many years before, there had been a bright wintry New England day, the weekend after New Year's. Hal and I had gone to investigate off-season Provincetown on Cape Cod in the middle of a cold snap. Going out from home base, the usual forty-five-minute flight had taken only a whizzing half hour, winds being smartly on our tail at cruising altitude. The return two days later found wind velocity cranked up to another level. We called Flight Service to get a weather briefing and file a VFR cross-country flight plan. Noting the anemometer readout at a drugstore registering a hair-raising top sixty-five knots, we figured we'd have to stay another day or two till things let up. But Flight Service (FSS) assured me that reading had to have captured a Venturi effect off the roof—winds in our area were reported at only twenty-five knots.

So we filed, went to the airport, and got ourselves nearly knocked off our feet by the wind gusts. Not good. Through the window of the locked-up lobby of summertime Provincetown-Boston Airlines, we squinted at their anemometer—and saw the same forty-five- to-sixty-five-knot reading. In the near zero cold, we did a stiff-fingered preflight, checked again with FSS, and got the same reassurance. In gusty winds, we gingerly taxied out and, angling across the runway to minimize the strong crosswind, applied the brakes, gave her full throttle, and then released her to surge forward. Even as a wind from the side, the headwind component was still strong.

We had liftoff barely before the moment we could have been blown off the side of the runway. As soon as the wheels came off the ground, I quickly turned into the wind and raised the nose, and up we soared. At two thousand feet, I radioed to open our flight plan. FSS responded, alarmed, "Do you have SIGMET Alpha One (alphanumeric significant meteorology report) for winds and turbulence in New England?" I had pithy words for him. Glancing behind for the airport, it was not there. Hal tapped my shoulder and pointed straight down. Holy cow. After climbing to two thousand feet, the runway was still directly under us. We had shot up like an elevator—or like kite on a string. At sixty-five hundred feet, it all smoothed out, no turbulence. But clearly, our short trip back wasn't going to be so short. My scalp prickled. Crossing the water back to the mainland . . . did I have enough gas? A quick calculation told me I did. I again called Flight Service, extending our ETA—by an hour.

The flight finally took a grindingly slow two and a half hours. We were thirty minutes overdue, and FSS was in a high-speed wobble looking for us. I was amused. They were worried big time about the girl and the lousy briefing they had given. But I knew better anyway. I had gotten out the Koch chart and POH (Pilots Operating Handbook) and figured I and the plane could handle it— and we did. I took risks, but I always knew my parameters. Maybe close to the edge, but never beyond.

SO WE TAKE OFF . . .

With a boosting headwind, we climbed like startled larks, flew the kilometers south to the coast, and then drifted eastward along the Great Australian Bight.

"Where are you, Reggie?"

"I'm just over the cliffs—where are you, Jerry?" We didn't want to run into each other. We banked our wings and peered down skyscraper-like precipices—knife-edged cliffs that stretched like a ribbon, fading far into the distance, blurred by sea mist. Rolling waves pounded them relentlessly, cliffs handsomely layered with multiple levels of strata, a geological baklava. Thick clouds of yellow sand boiled out at the base into brilliant cobalt-blue tides, mesmerizing, the cliff line guiding us to the head of the Bight.

"Oh I see you now, Jerry! I'll sidle over the land so you can come in closer for a good picture." It was like that. When flying, we often lost sight of each other, and we were glad to have the radio for position reports.

At the head, some mama whales were still fleshing out their calves for the long haul to the Antarctic. They kept them snug into the shoreline, where they were more protected and where the best feeding is. We counted fifteen pods, a lot, we thought—but actually most had gone on. We felt lucky to have seen any. Our timing was off . . . too late in the season for the big show. Earlier, the tally had been eighty.

So we turned toward Ceduna, located on the Eyre Peninsula, the town known as the gateway to the Nullarbor. (Ceduna is a corruption of the local Aboriginal word

"Chedoona" meaning "place to sit down and rest." Well, okay, we can do that.) Flying over increasingly agricultural territory, we saw the Nullarbor morph into fertile lands. Ceduna is a major highway crossing and an important southern coastal railway hub. Tracks and industrial tanks helped us home in on the little port town and its dirt strip. No interesting winds at this end of the leg. Good. Gusty landings are trickier than windy takeoffs.

Passing over the Great Australian Bight, defined by dramatic cliffs

After landing rollout, an alarming big blue-tongued lizard waddled menacingly up to us on the airstrip. We stopped to gawk. His tongue-flicking approach sent us gunning our engine to the ramp. Turns out he was merely curious; some insist there are no poisonous lizards in Australia. So? They still like to bite. And if the goanna is perhaps not actually venomous (the debate goes on there), their mouths are filthy and full of germs that can infect and kill you.

We made our way to light-aircraft parking and off-loaded, hunching our shoulders against panicky dive-bombing plovers. They were protecting their ramp-edge nests. Whiz, bob, and run for it! Lots more threatening than our killdeers, the US airport (and golf course) nesters that do the broken-wing routine to lure danger from their foolish ground nests. (Gravel is their favorite. They plop their eggs down on camouflaging pebbles.)

Transport arrived from the East West Motel, our overnight full-service accommodation. But luncheon hours were over. It's our karma . . . we arrive too late for lunch. Across the road we snacked at a nice little café and then settled back into our rooms.

Reggie and Brad had tuned in their TV to catch a rough-and-tough Aussie Rugby League game, and we got invited in for some indoctrination. It was a wild Manly versus Sydney cliff-hanger. Brad hailed from Manly, so we cheerfully barracked that team. (Not "rooted for.") One lad nearly got his neck snapped, a horribly contorted sight. Rugby is as rough as it gets. (Manly lost.)

The East West Motel, strangely enough, so far away from any metropolitan influence (the largest and nearest would be Adelaide, almost five hundred miles to its southeast) served us the best tour cuisine yet. For a remote town of four thousand, it was a surprising culinary jewel, thanks to a great chef. Ceduna's main industries are grain shipping, fishing—and harvesting that splendid Pacific oyster. After a gustatorily robust dinner that included those succulent oysters, we played some desultory pool and then hit the sack—there wasn't much going on in Ceduna. Once a year though, Ceduna holds a giant oyster fest that attracts up to six thousand fanatics—alas, not on our beat.

But all in all, it had been a fine Sunday.

25 ONWARD TO BROKEN HILL

MORNING, THE NEXT DAY . . .

Ceduna departure—our start-up weather was snivelly and gray, but after refueling the day cleared to acceptable VFR. Nick dressed our propeller blade (filed smooth the prop edges to keep dangerous cracks from starting). It had probably been dinged by a stone whisked up during the WA/SA takeoff. It was then "All stations Ceduna, etc. . . . " the required pretakeoff taxiing announcement for departure—no goanna in our path—and off we soared to a place curiously called Broken Hill, via a Port Augusta fuel stop. We're managing our fuel well—we're now using only 10.5 gallons per hour, not bad for our beefed up engine.

We climbed to ninety-five hundred feet for the grand overview and headed eastward past farm fields to landscapes uplifted and contorted during the earth's primordial boil. SCU's windows were dully yellowed, so to fully appreciate the geology and its colors we had to open them up. That's one of the delights of the Cessna 172 . . . it can fly at airspeeds slow enough to open windows. But then the cabin gets unpleasantly breezy, so you slow down and lose arrival time.

JUMP PLANE . . . "IF IT CAIN'T KILL YOU, IT AIN'T A SPORT"

Slow-moving aircraft can bore well through the air, without doors—although that causes aerodynamic changes and a bit of good airstreaming speed is lost. Stall speeds are altered and so forth, rather like an old-timey open cockpit. (FAA permission and documentation are required for any modification to the original certification.) When my airport's manager asked me if I would be willing to drop parachute jumpers into some fairgrounds, I allowed as how yes, I believed I would. Oh yes, yes indeed. A new bright thread to weave into what I call my life's tapestry. I took the doors off my plane, but first went to the area FAA office for the permit papers.

Daybreak came; it was country-fair dazzling, light winds fore-

casted—we were good to go. Eagerly I welcomed the jumpers on board. They had brought me my own chute to wear . . . the pilot must also be so equipped—"just in case." God forbid, what if somebody's chute catches and tangles on the plane? We could all spiral to our deaths. Have to be able to jump well away from it. All jumpers positioned properly in the cabin, poised, tensed, and ready, off we went. Slowly lumbering upward, heavy, with extra jumper weight slowing the aircraft, circling on up to the release altitude of ten thousand feet.

On the climb, we surveyed crowds below, clustered around striped tents. At some strategic point the jumpers tossed out a long crepe paper streamer, a wind-drift indicator. All eyes were riveted on its slow flutter down, noting the slight sideways direction it took. A huge X in a big circle marked the target landing spot. The streamer settled near it. They guesstimated the distance and degrees, crepe paper to big X. Roaring noisy in the cabin, they used hand gestures to communicate, and then finally, they gave me the thumbs-up when I should let them out, one at a time. Just a moment before each jump, I had to skid the plane, angling the tail to the side, positioning myself so that as the flight continued forward the jumper would not be struck by the tail section's horizontal stabilizer.

As they leaped out one by one, hurtling swiftly toward the ground, I thought darkly, "So long, fools!" and peered after them, circling the target, watching anxiously for their bright billowing parachutes. I mean, what if? . . . Please God, not these guys—not on my beat! But okay . . . there were the chutes, gently drifting, no longer hurtling. But how could anyone ever jump out of a perfectly safe airplane—for kicks? To prove bravery and machismo to each other and the world? To get girls? Like dogs to the dinner whistle, girls flock to risk-taking sports heroes ("Ooh, Johnny you're so brave!") Yeah, that's right. "If it cain't kill you—it ain't a sport."

PORT AUGUSTA

Australia is a macho sporting country, and the people love their excitement. So like many places in Australia, Port Augusta, too, offered skydiving, or parachute jumping. But that wasn't our agenda. We just stopped for a quick top-off.

The area was a center for gypsum mining. Slowly it appeared in the midst of an impressively blossoming desert. The lands below us had just been washed with nurturing rain. Along with bunches of wild onion, thick patches of purple covered many areas on roadsides and taxiways, along with yellow wattle acacia. That showy purple is called Patterson's Curse, a prolific vivid wildflower—miserably toxic to animals—a weed pest that aggressively takes over paddocks and grazing lands. In these less arid parts of Western and Southern Australia, it was in strikingly lovely peak bloom. This purple flowering plant originated in Europe. In the late eighteen hundreds, a Mr. Patterson planted it in his garden in Sydney—and oh heavens to Betsy, didn't it spread. It became a wretched invasive curse (ergo the name).

Except to apiary enthusiasts. It's a fine bee magnet.

The Port Augusta fueling concession was handled by their aero club. After taking on our needed petrol, off we went, climbing out to first circle over the city's huge gypsum factory. It had so many lines going to it that it looked like a power plant.

That done, we continued up, leveled off at seventy-five hundred feet to clear the en route Flinders Ranges —and a broken cloud deck. What we could not see, but knew were there, were ridgetops obscured by clouds. Why you don't scud run near mountains. (Dry aviation humor: the cloud covering the rocky peak is dubbed "cumulo-granite." Big nasty thunderstorm? "Nympho-cumulus." You figure it out.)

Eventually clouds and emerald greens below disappeared behind us, our passage now bringing us to views of rich ochers and reds, tracking the leg to our next stop, Broken Hill. We were to spend two days in this home of the once-largest silver mine in the world. No longer the biggest, it still yields lead, zinc, and yes, silver. We would do a deep mine tour on the first day.

Oh goody.

26 BROKEN HILL

OUR FLIGHT THROUGH CLEAR skies to Broken Hill delivered us to a fine view of its mine and, after landing, transport to our Miners Lamp Motel gave us a good look at the town via a serendipitous detour around a funeral procession. We opted to be happy for the chance, instead of annoyed by the inconvenience.

The town and mine took their name out of English explorer Charles Sturt's journals. Sturt (born in India, educated at Harrow) had attempted (like Burke and Wills) to find good central rivers on the Australian continent; the surveying and naming of the Murray and Darling rivers can be credited to his efforts. Sturt viewed the vast plains of Australia and recommended development by the British, who subsequently granted him an enormous tract for himself. He continued his explorations, coming and going occasionally from England. In 1844 he noted in his journals, his chronicling of his trekkings, the observation of an irregular, broken-looking hill in the Barrier Range. Forty years later, silver ore was discovered at this site. But by now, vigorous mining had erased those contours from the map.

Broken Hill's history and architecture are said to be the boldest of the outback (during all its past, Broken Hill flagrantly defied government-decreed bar closing hours—you can tipple whenever). Its buildings ranged from stunning palatial old Federation and Victorian styles and 1930s art deco edifices, to classic tin cottages. These all made our entry here wonderfully surprising. We had no idea a mining town in the middle of apparent desolation would be so interesting. But then, why not? This was Australia! There was a lot of silver to be had—and that meant opulence. It was here that the biggest silver mine in the world operated for years, bringing wealth to more than a few. BHP, the Broken Hill Proprietary Company, nicknamed "the Big Australian," was huge.

The Miners Lamp had its own lively pub, already filled with hardworking, thirsty miners. We unwound there for a while, faded for a quick doze, arose later for a Chinese dinner in the dining room. (Australians love Chinese food.) An exchange of salty jokes and Dr. Lie Chee again set us howling. A postdinner stroll around town before bedtime. Always a good settling-down plan after a feast. And we had surely feasted.

And bedtime was not appealing. I was worried.

Pulling up the covers, I lay there brooding about the next day's deep mine tour, headline-making tunnel collapses darkening my thoughts, my eyes boring holes in the gloom. You know what? I'm much happier up in the sky than down under the ground. I made up my mind. I just was not going . . .

. . . but I did.

THE MINE

The day dawned fair and fine—not that we were going to see much of it down underground. I shuddered. Early in the day, no time to dwell on it, off we went. Arriving at the mine, they quickly, efficiently squished us into a twenty-passenger cage elevator—no wasted space—the switch was flipped and down we sank, shaking and rattling through a dimly lit shaft. We off-loaded into a large, pleasantly non-claustrophobic tunnel. "Non," if you think only of space, not of overhead ground pressure tonnage. Well, I knew I wasn't safe . . . So I really couldn't pay much attention to the historical and engineering data delivered by the tour guide, standing around shifting from foot to foot. Reggie growled and said the guide was a "blooming communist." He did bore us to yawns with a tirade about the world's mining machinery putting folks out of work. Too bad. Hey, it was a hole dug to pull out goodies.

Tour done, the return to the surface was quite nerve fraying, squeezed into that box cage, all facing forward, breath on each others' necks. Never mind, I made it down, I could do it again—especially to get up to the surface and whiz chop-chop away from there. I could hear the creaking and grinding of the cage's gear mechanisms, and then, oh God, the light went out. A wave of terror rose from my gut. An elevator breakdown? I shuddered and gasped out, "Oh no, we're trapped!" A woman's hand reached over from behind and grasped my shoulder, and miraculously, my fear vanished. Wow. How did she know to do that? What a sweet sudden kindness from an invisible stranger. The elevator kept lumbering upward, but in darkness.

The bulb had probably burned out.

Ground level came with a jerking stop, the cage door opened—in poured light and out poured people—especially me. I looked around for my guardian angel who grinned as she caught my eye—I flashed profound thanks.

CULTURE

The area's scope reached far beyond the mine, in this middle of nowhere. Although well distanced from regular civilization, it was hardly a cultural wasteland. Broken Hill and its region bustled with sophistication. The arts were alive, both literary and visual. A talented band of authors (e.g., Kenneth Cook and crime writer Arthur Upfield), the artists' group Brushmen of the Bush (including Pro Hart and Jack Absalom), Australian New Wave moviemakers (Australian New Wave seminal films: *Wake in Fright* and later *The Adventures of Priscilla, Queen of the Desert*) . . . and countryside sculpture parks. We keenly anticipated checking all of it out—a lot for a two-day stopover, but we would gear up and have at it.

For our layover, Brad rented a twelve-year-old Ford, loaded us in, all but Nick who had other business to attend to, and merrily sped out through scrubby lands bursting with springtime flowers, spotting leaping wallabies and kangaroos—out of town to colorful offbeat places, some of national interest. After the excursion into the mine, over the rest of the two days we did a comprehensive sprint through all the other good things. First, the ghost mining town, Silverton, once threaded with a fat silver lode. Silverton was the erstwhile home to some of the nineteenth century's silver-rich, but now it was a tiny settlement of artists and galleries. We then visited painter Pro Hart's city-located permanent art collection.

Then to the best—the Living Desert Sculpture Site, miles out in the countryside.

The Desert Sanctuary was an exceptional attraction: many handsome creations of local stone, results of an innovative sculpture symposium. By invitation, sculptors had gathered from parts afar to flex creative muscles, chiseling out their designs from large desert boulders. They pitched work tents and camped on-site for two weeks to do it. The results were impressive, exciting—and some, just plain fun.

Then the finale. Like a silent crescendo the day's end powered up, its magnitude so unexpected. The site's hilltop sunset slowly intensified, and as night began to rise, distant mountains became sculpted by beams racing across the plains. Purple peaks rose beyond wide fields of desert flowers; we scrambled up to join others who had come from Broken Hill just to see this. The sweeping horizon was a stage. The sun hovered on its rim in an intense, vivid flameout, a red-end spectrum that shifted to cobalt—a near-mystical thing, there on that faraway desert.

For our last night in Broken Hill, Nick had arranged dinner for us at the Social Democratic Club, one of those private dining and gambling clubs customary in Australian towns—places where you sign on tear sheets as the guest of somebody in order to drink and eat in attractive surroundings.

Later, to shake down a little of the feedbag, we walked back to the Miners Lamp.

Tomorrow, we fly to a place "older than dirt."

27 MUNGO LAKE

PREPARING FOR THE CHILLY southeast, we hauled out fleece jackets, leaving our mining town in the warm dust to visit ancient Lake Mungo—a prehistoric Aboriginal outpost. We cruised down low, the 130-mile flight at an average altitude of five hundred feet—good for sighting prospectors' diggings and noting the emergence of new types of eucalyptus—and the reemergence of that intriguing spinifex, a brush that grows in doughnut-like rings. Flat lands led us to flatter lands, bringing us to ancient lake beds. These were drained for agricultural use and ingeniously arranged to flood for watering. In the distance, we eventually spied the sandy "lunette" of the enormous dry lake and Mungo Lodge's handy airport—not to be confused with the bigger National Park airstrip.

Midday thermals were busily mushrooming, inserting wild wind-shear lifts and sinks to our carefully planned approaches and giving unsettling, "This way! No, that way!" behavior to the wind sock. Never mind; we greased her on. Love those forgiving dirt strips, even though we've had to have a few gravel prop dings filed out. Nick said this propeller would be dumped when the engine is overhauled. Normal maintenance, flying the outback.

Lake Mungo gives pithy meaning to the saying "older than dirt." In its lunette, a gigantic gently sloped sand dune with an arced high ridge delineating its boundaries (new-moon shaped, ergo the name) they've found artifacts that date back at least forty thousand years. Some archeologists think that humans may have trekked across these lands as long as 120,000 years ago.

Handsomely ringed by Murray pines and the kind of fencing you'd tie a horse to (good for feeling your way back to your cabin after dark) the mountain-lodge type rustic-beamed building and its outbuildings were right there at the airstrip. We made our way to its deck and scarfed up sandwiches. The lodge was also a conference center, equipped with a van for our use. Brad commandeered it, grabbing up brochures and maps, herding us onward—this time, guide Nick was at the wheel.

It was an afternoon of learning—about how the Aborigine, in the near dawn of time, had already developed to the point of cooking in clay stoves (creatively reusing termite mounds) and had special burial rites—one for men (cremation) and another for women. How long could it have taken to evolve to that state? We just couldn't wrap our minds around that one. We climbed and toured the lunette, a formation here and there wind-molded and rain-carved into wonderful shapes, stretching several miles into a long crescent mound rimming one side of the dry lake bed—dry now, for an estimated fifteen thousand years. Tiny fossils caught our eyes, glinting in the sand; experts needed to unravel which bit was what.

Emus and kangaroos played in the scrub on either side of the dunes, and special roads had been built to lead the curious into areas of mallee (clever eucalyptus that sprouts several narrow trunks up and outward from one center to conduct rainwater downward to the soil at its middle, shedding leaves to form a mat that will shade and hold the moisture, solely for the mallee's own use). And here was saltbush—a thick, silver-leafed shrub that indeed tasted salty.

Australia is the Dr. Seuss book of continents. Flitting among the trees we sighted ever-present magpies and rosy galahs, random flashy ring-necked parrots, and a new kind of sweet-voiced honeyeater. Kangaroos seemed to want to play crazy with cars. They would wait till we were motoring and then bound out right in front of us, virtually playing chicken. The desert had recently received good seasonal rains, and a lacy veil of wildflowers spread the land with life and color—surface-hugging tiny white star blossoms, saturated yellow wattles, and miscellaneous other yellow blooms.

Nick pointed out a genuinely nasty insect—the giant tan and black bull ant. He explained that they have a little hair-like stinger that injects—and reinjects—vicious stinging venom. He claimed they are smart enough to sneak around behind you to attack. We didn't test that out. We hotfooted away before we could find out.

The lodge came equipped with an irresistible pool table where we shared lighthearted moments before dinner. A hearty New England-style boiled feast lured us into the great room with its blazing fireplace. Jerry was getting sick, so he faded before his cherished dessert—the family cold was starting its rounds. Reggie followed his own credo and killed his with alcohol. Hal and I, so far, were not afflicted.

Fun falling into place as it will, that rollicking round of pool resumed during dessert. The last crumb lapped up, we went out into the nighttime—and groped our way to our cabins. No outside lights. Inching our way along the fencing, using the one flashlight one of us had snatched from a plane, we found our beds. But not before we stood, awestruck, to take in the stars, thick and brilliant. No light pollution. The night was stunning, tomb-silent. It was too nippy even for insect rustlings. Something as vast and splendid as that sky should have sound. We were again on the deck of our starship, eyes searching the universe.

There was cozy gas heat in the cabin for sleeping well. Good thing. Tomorrow's start to the wine country will be early.

28 MUDGEE AND WINERIES

*"Age is irrelevant—unless, of course, you happen
to be a bottle of wine."*

—Joan Collins

THE AUSSIES HAVE BEEN producing wines
since the early eighteen hundreds. Immigrants brought in
cuttings from the best of Europe's stock to establish top-
notch wines of all types in places like Western Australia's
Margaret River, the Barossa Valley in South Australia, and
Mudgee in the Great Dividing Range of NSW (New South
Wales). We were getting ready to go sample a few in wine-
prosperous Mudgee—extant since 1858.

Early start—off we taxied from outside our cabins, lined
up for takeoff, mentally prepared for headwinds, staying
low to minimize their effect. The drag from the earth's
surface slows the wind's velocity at low altitude—the more
you don't climb into that headwind, the better time you'll
make.

We flew along exhilaratingly low, out there where nobody lived. The noisy aircraft baffled emus, jump-started kangaroos, and skittered nervous sheep. And we got to peer fairly close up at the curious spinifex. One way we oriented ourselves in this nearly featureless region—on our GPSs and charts we checked off lines of latitude and longitude.

Flying toward the fertile Cudgegong River Valley to find Mudgee ("nest in the hills") the landscape became lined with shining canals as it became agricultural. Needing fuel en route, we homed in on Griffith, a town in an area of fragrant citrus orchards and vineyards, in the important Murrumbidgee Irrigation Area. Griffith had been laid out by landscape architect Walter Burley Griffin from Chicago; he also designed Canberra.

After fill-ups, we taxied for takeoff past sweeping yellow carpets of wildflowers, soaring off to our wine country stopover.

Climbing to seventy-five hundred feet, we left bumpy turbulence behind. Better winds now—our groundspeed picked up. But a deck started forming beneath us, so down we went again, before it closed in.

Mudgee's airport ramp was showing two DC-3s, known there as Dakotas, with "Royal Mail" emblazoned on them—special outing planes to bring people for vineyard visits. Oh yes, we are now in wine country. That's what Mudgee is all about.

Australians are more than beer drinkers. There's a large group of savvy oenophiles emerging from their superior wine industry. The climate and soil in those regions is prime for grapes.

"LIFE IS TOO SHORT TO DRINK BAD WINE" (ANONYMOUS)

Our tour got off to an ignominious start: a mead winery/brewery. Honey beer or honey wine, the ancient drink. Perhaps it's an acquired taste. We did enjoy the lecture on its history and processing.

The next stop was our kind of vineyard, one that produced organic, unadulterated wines. Superb wines, untainted by preservatives, part of an up-and-coming but still-fringe market. We thought we might find room in a suitcase for a bottle or two.

The biggest Mudgee vineyard had huge fermenting barrels in cave-like structures. Sight always influencing palates, those rolled beautifully over the tongue. Many stops, many samplings. The palate was amused, but maybe stressed? We bought a few carefully selected bottles. That luggage thing. Those tastings were not unsuprisingly soporific; we returned to our rooms and flopped. Morpheus smiled.

All napped out, we arose to feast at the Lawson Park Hotel and Grill, big handsome pub on one side, grill on the other. You get your drink, join the fray, grill your own steak. Great fun. Prime meat, lovely vegetables, a favorite place with locals. We sipped while searing and turning fillets together, happily accepting good-humored advice.

The chatty cabbie back to our hotel, pleasant but wryly cynical, gave us his handout poem about what a taxi man sees. It's in the appendix.

The next day, on to seaside Port Macquarie—our last stop before the end. And we're going to have to go cold turkey when we wind up this grand adventure.

We try not to think about it. It rots.

29 PORT MACQUARIE

ANOTHER FAIR DAY, PERFECT for our flight to the coast. Our van man came to haul us, along with his preschool kids—bachelor Reggie cowered in the back, muttering about "ferals." They did have an irritating presence—all those decibels and energy.

A crystal-clear passage over the Great Dividing Range—with coveted tailwinds. And o-kay! There's the east-side ocean again. Counting down . . .

Port Macquarie materialized on the meandering Hastings River. Quickly we were parked and looking for gas. That turned out to be a process requiring the airport operator's own special slide card—which of course we did not have. Cash only, for us.

That settled, a wildly rocking cab ride took us into town, a two-cab arrangement—our driver racing frantically to keep up with the one who knew the way.

Port Macquarie was a sparkling port town with not-surprising threats of new shoreline condos and the unsurprising hue and cry against them. We were on the "against" side ourselves, deeming it rude and unfair to put high-rises in front of everyone else, blotting out their lovely water view.

Oops—our motel, the six-story Mid Pacific Motel, was smack on the waterfront. What the heck. Somebody had to be in those lovely intrusive rooms, no? It was already built. We were assigned fine rooms with great views.

Once settled, we headed out for the Riverside Terrace, a chic waterside luncheon place. "Have the Brown Brothers cab sauv," advised waiter John. "I'll bring a crunchy bread damper." A damper is table bread that hearkens back to swagmen and drovers' bread, cooked in the ashes of their campfires. Sometimes it comes baked in little clay flowerpots. We spent a lovely couple of hours, sipping wine, munching luncheon squid on farfalle with white wine cream sauce and then tamped in a Thai salad generously loaded with seared rare beef strips. Idly watching, as we dined, passing boats in the harbor.

Hal pulled out our binoculars. Hmm. Rental boats?

Well, why not rent one? Up the street at Tourist Information, they booked us a boat and hailed a cab to get us to the marina. On approach to the cab, two surly louts tried to grab it from us. Ha! It was Reggie and Brad, pulling our legs. Big hoots and laughs—and bravo, they joined us for our Hastings River adventure.

Our canopied boat sported faded lettering that said "Bessie." Well okay, Bessie—let's have at it. She took us up the waterway, first showing us pelicans, looking totally unairworthy but coasting effortlessly over the water, one of them taunting a dolphin, clearing it by an inch. They had those expressionless flat black eyes. They were scanning for tidbits.

Followed by pelicans and the odd dolphin, we puttered along, checking out waterside residences. Nice lifestyle. After boating—a cheery pub stop. Beer flowed from oddly white, fat taps and beer pulls—thick frost buildup from the humid seaside air.

Then back to those nifty rooms, a shower, and short rests before dinner. It had been a grand afternoon.

Nick had planned a special farewell dinner for us at the attractive Al Dente gourmet Italian place overlooking the harbor, just down the block. And so we gathered. But where was Jerry? We waited. And waited.

He had been such a question mark. Finally Nick went back and had the hotel check out his room. Maybe he was ill—or perhaps simply showering? Nope—he wasn't there. Nick left a message in the empty room.

During coffee and reminiscences, Nick gave us a fun trip quiz, charming certificates, and golden wing pins; and then out of nowhere, Jerry appeared. Cheers of relief. What had happened? I had been about to report him missing. Well—not getting the message about our dinner, he had gone off and eaten on his own. But he came supplied with some great photos he had taken and developed that afternoon. As I said at the outset, Jerry was one of a kind. I believe he was sorry to miss our final dinner, pleased that we had been concerned about him. But who could really tell.

Tomorrow would be our last day, our last flyabout leg. A melancholy thought.

30 REDCLIFFE

CIRCUMNAVIGATOR CLOSES ITS CIRCLE

It was the last day of our adventure, our circumnavigation. What a good choice, the stop at Port Macquarie. Dramatic, the difference between the west coast and the east coast. We had earlier explored sprawling Sydney and the Brisbane area—this time we got an important look-see at Australia's beguiling coastal living. And the stop gave us a chance to debrief before the end.

Brekkie came to our rooms (we love the way they do that—even if there's no in-house coffee shop, they always get you going with some breakfast) and then we were off again in a taxi—the same one that had taken us to-and-from the rental boat jaunt. He practically felt like an old friend.

I would be pilot in command going to Redcliffe. I pushed for Hal to take the leg. Since I had flown out at start-up, it seemed fair that he should fly back in. But he wasn't having it.

The takeoff went well, but shortly we had a problem.

The GPS became lifeless—not a flicker. Just after making the coastline, it took a walk. Now what? At Nick's radioed instruction, we landed at Kempsey so he could see about it. A GPS was a necessity to navigate around the Coolangatta MBZ, farther up the line. It would be some sort of insanity to try and fly the crowded coastline without proper avionics, especially since we were strangers. Like wandering clueless through the complicated Los Angeles Basin.

Oh blast—the battery was flat. Not a twitch of action. The GPS apparently had been running on battery for quite a while—its plug-in to the panel was loose, not recharging. This model Garmin had no "low bat" warning function. Nick muttered under his breath, tinkered with the lighter housing, made it come alive—and off we went.

Gamely we executed the busy controlled airspace airway clearance up the coast through Coffs Harbour. (Controller: "Report Nambucca Heads"), MBZ'd the Ballina airspace, hastily cast an eye over scenic rivers and estuaries when we could—navigating landmarks needed all of our attention, and cruised into the outskirts of Coolie (Coolangatta) according to Nick's preplanned strategy.

(Oh, a goody about Coolangatta. After the end, we got a condo rental in Surfers Paradise and tootled down the coast to Coolie's airport to round up some charts and do some seaside noshing. We found a place that had phenomenal oyster shooters built with a special sake and a light touch of wasabi. I still dream of them.)

To keep safely out of the busy Coolangatta Class B, we cautiously tucked a bit west of our northerly course-line, finding rippling foothills reaching up to meet us as we stayed below the floor of the approach corridor. Not much margin for clearance—low scuddy clouds contraindicated any further westerly deviation over the mountains. It was fun, slipping over ridges where large snugged-in houses filled the requirement of highest and best use of that steep-pitched land, checking out top-drawer homes with commanding ocean views. Not quite the exhilaration of hedgehopping, but still great fun. Hillsides much like California's bay areas. It was another facet of dazzling Australia . . . A world away from the kangaroo hopping, spinifex-scattered dry lands we had not long ago flown over.

Then the visibility dropped to skunk in smoke and pollution; the Gold Coast practically disappeared, as we groped our way to the VFR coastal corridor. We never were sure we even saw the city of Southport while staying clear of the busy bits. Marginal? The visibility was scandalous.

Our VTC (the paper aeronautical chart) got soft and well thumbed as we pawed and sweated on it, peering for confirming landmarks. The VTC was the Bible here—though we did rely heavily on the GPS. And so we wove our way home via Moreton Island (the westerly crossover point) and back to Redcliffe. There were a few more whale sightings in the bay, just to rub in the sting of ending.

And so, back to where we started.

Such a joyful family reunion. For Nick's family, it had been a trying month's separation accented with such unpleasant events. But somewhere during our trip's kaleidoscope, Nick's wife's tests proved her healthy, good meds had licked Nick's infection, and the Danes' disaster was looking more redeemable. That had all helped. And now—after the tense last leg through low visibility—we were delighted to relax and tuck into a crispy and succulent

welcome-back rooster chicken feast. And what nice, nice
kids Nick had. Such a better grade of child than the ferals,
the ones that had horrified Reggie.

The planes got battened down, and we said our wistful
"Maybe see you next trip?" farewells and got loaded up and
transported out.

Rooster chicken is great—but cold turkey is for the
birds. It would be hard to readjust.

In a few days, Qantas had once again carried us up and
over the Intertropical Convergence Zone. Now we were
two hours out of Los Angeles. But back in Sydney, there
had been a delay. Looking out at our awaiting flight from
the gate's windows, we had observed a disturbing stream
of fuel pour from one wing tank. Maintenance scrambled
like a fire drill. It had been set right, and the fuel cleaned
up. We were now many hours into our return flight, two
hours from landing, and I was contentedly sitting in a
jump seat up front with the pilots. They were giving me
a quick overview of the then-new high-tech glass panel
instrumentation. The captain was explaining the redun-
dancy of the 747's displays, glass panel versus the old
gauges.

"How much fuel do we have?" he asked, pointing to the
fancy new gauge readouts on the console.

"Oh!" I gasped in confusion. "It says zero . . . that's
none!" My skin prickled.

"No worries," calmly responded the copilot. "We
couldn't get the new ones to reset after the fuel fix. See the
old gauges? They still work."

My eyes sought them out, finding them in a tier of dials

above the windscreen. With profound relief I saw that we had nearly one-quarter of the fuel left—more than enough for the rest of the trip.

And so into LAX, where old pilot friends came to meet us, helping with bags—easing us into readjustment to our land's northern latitudes. No more "Strahlian" in our ears, no more left-side driving.

But those woolly coats? Not yet.

Afterword

What's on *your* bucket list?

This trip to Australia, our second of three, took place in 1997. When Hal retired, we were up for adventuring, something this aero tour had already supplied abundantly before. Aviator Nick has since closed his tour business, but others have replaced him. Since I don't know those firsthand, I can't advocate for or against any of them. But I can enthusiastically recommend Australia—and especially seeing it by light personal airplane. If you are already a pilot, doing so should be high on your list of things to do.

If you are not—but the urge to become one is in your blood—it's a good reason to learn.

Postscript

Air Force Brat Years

DO LADIES FLY, MOMMY?

As a child of the military, my early years were spent wide-eyed, moving about the world´s checkerboard of exotic places. Those were happy times, following my Air Force father to the Philippines, Japan, Europe, and coast to coast all over America. My southern gentlewoman mother kept me close by at her knee, imparting her kind of wisdom as I grew up. When I once asked her, "Do ladies fly, Mommy?" Mama said, "Well, I suppose a few women do, but they are mannish and wear army boots . . . not our kind."

Several years later we were stationed in Paris. I was a poised, soignée, slightly affected sweet sixteen. It was all show, of course. I was still a childish tomboy, sneaking onto rooftops wherever we lived. I always liked the high overview, which our steep slate Paris roof made me rethink—scared me witless, slipping along those shingles. There was a reception at the US air attaché's elegant Saint-

Cloud hilltop mansion in that Paris suburb, all set about with broad lawns and trailing arbors, a misty romantic view of nearby Paris spread out at its feet. The affair was a tented soiree in honor of the beautiful and famous aviatrix Jacqueline Cochran, coordinator of the famous WASPs, Women's Airforce Service Pilots. Cochran was a tough but glamorous woman. In her early career days, preaviation, she had established a cosmetics company. Now here she was, swish in a chic satin gown. (I thought her overdressed, really.) I experienced a startling eye-opener. Here was a woman pilot, and—I noted—she definitely wasn't wearing army boots.

I was the only teen there, but the air attaché, a good friend of my parents, liked me and apparently thought I could hold my own with Ms. Cochran—and add some youth to the occasion. Remember, young women had been her *métier* while recruiting for the WASPs. (In later years I met a sassy one who had lied her way into the corps at sixteen.) White-jacketed waiters passed trays of drinks and canapés. We were introduced. Relieved by the diversion, officers' wives fled as if we had a bad rash—it appeared they were intimidated by her mojo and accomplishments way outside their ken. After trading a few requisite platitudes, she coolly eyed my sixteen-year-old self and asked me if I was a pilot. Me, what, fly? Flummoxed, I looked down and away. I was merely receiving-line mature—I was truly feckless and unformed. When I said no, she swished off to seek someone more interesting, mildly chastising me that maybe I should.

I found my mother. I said, "She's beautiful, isn't she?" Mama pinched her lips together and squeezed out a yes. The seed was planted.

Military drifting did nothing to establish roots, which I wistfully thought I missed and needed. But sand was well and good in my shoes, and forever after I needed to go . . . wherever. Genetic? Maybe. After all, our country was settled by the restless.

I imagine it was inevitable. One day, years after learning to fly—off I went to ramble the world, bit by bit. And I wanted to share some of it with you, tell you how it was.

Especially flying in Australia.

APPENDIX

Waltzin' Matilda,
by Banjo (A. B.) Patterson

Once a jolly swagman camped beside a billabong
Under the shade of a coolibah tree,
And he sang as he watched and waited till his billy boiled,
   "You'll come a-waltzin' Matilda with me."

Refrain:

Waltzin' Matilda, waltzin' Matilda,
You'll come a-waltzin' Matilda with me
And he sang as he watched and waited till his billy boiled,
   "You'll come a waltzin' Matilda with me."

Down came a jumbuck to drink at that billabong;
Up jumped the swagman and grabbed him with glee.
And he sang as he stuffed that jumbuck in his tucker bag,
   "You'll come a-waltzin' Matilda with me."

Refrain:

Up rode the squatter, mounted on his thoroughbred;
Down came the troopers, one, two, three.
"Who's that jolly jumbuck you've got in your tucker bag?
    You'll come a-waltzin' Matilda with me."

Refrain:

Up jumped the swagman and sprang into the billabong.
"You'll never catch me alive," said he.
And his ghost may be heard as you pass by that billabong:
    You'll come a-waltzin' Matilda with me.

THE CABBY
(Anonymous taxi driver's poem)

The taxi cab driver sits in his car,
He waits for calls from near and afar.
He knows all the crooks
And he knows all the rooks
He knows all the bad roads, he knows all the nooks.
He knows all the girls who are chasing the boys
He knows all our troubles, he knows all our strife
And he knows every man who ducks out
from his wife.
If a taxicab driver told even half what he knows
He would turn all our friends
into bitterest foes.
He would sow a small wind that
would soon be a gale,
Engulf us in trouble and land us in gaol.
He would start forth a story which,

Gaining in force
Would cause half the wives to sue for divorce.
He would get all our homes mixed up in fights
And turn our bright days
Into sorrowing nights.
In fact he would keep the whole town in a stew
If he told one-tenth of the things
That he knew.
So here's a hint—if you pay him his fees,
He won't know a thing but his A's, B's, and C's.

Author's Note

I'M TOLD SOME WILL wish to know about our son who died of cancer. In this book of adventurous discovery, a part of our recovery process, I will not detail his and our ordeal. This is a happy book, a book of good memories and of flying around Australia, including my special moments with Shona, who also lost a child. I believe we were meant to meet. I will not omit that part just to avoid getting into it. But enough terrible child deaths have been recounted. It's best for the human heart to get on with it, to learn however painfully to orbit the horrible black hole, and not be drawn into it.

David Graham, a dear Aero Club friend, advised, "Get back on the horse, Michelee. You must fly again." He was right. As I took to the skies after such a long time away, my instructor commiserated sadly and said, "It sure takes the starch out, doesn't it?" Big time. But skills were just waiting to be teased into action, and again I became that uplifting union of me, plane, sky. A source of happiness that has never failed me.

ABOUT THE AUTHOR

Born a Texan to a career Air Force officer and very Southern mother, Michelee spent her impressionable early years all around the world, on a path that brought her to a first marriage at twenty-one. Two children later, with useful time served volunteering at hospitals and museums, she found her way to her first flight lesson. In the ensuing nearly fifty years, she has since logged more than 5,000 hours of flight time, including these in Australia. She holds a commercial license (both single engine land and glider) with instrument rating, and a tow pilot endorsement, and has been active in several aviation organizations, including the volunteer Airlifeline (now Angel Flight).

Michelee has been married to her second husband, Harold Cabot, for more than 45 years, and is the mother of two wonderful children and three charming step-children. Her extended modern family includes a delightful array of dauthers and sons-in-law and clever, beautiful "grands"and "great-grands" that give her much pleasure. She has lived in Alamos, Mexico, with her husband Hal and their Cessna P210 for twelve years. When recently sitting on an aviation conference panel in Mumbai—a celebration of 100 years of India's Civil Aviation—someone asked "After all these years, why do you still fly?" The audience of pilots and controllers became a moving sea of nodding heads at her smiling answer—"Because I still need the overview." And she still flies today; she and her husband through the years have become a smoothly-tooled combo in the cockpit and, as in this Australian adventure, they are still swapping legs—and still loving the overview.

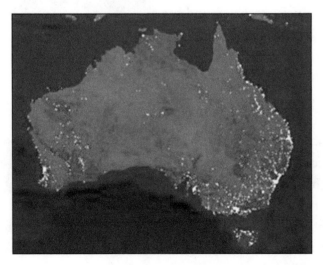

From Space—NASA

CPSIA information can be obtained
at www.ICGtesting.com
Printed in the USA
BVHW06s0319260618
520039BV00004B/6/P